INSTAGRAM INFLUENCER

HOW TO BUILD YOUR PERSONAL BRAND AND REACH ONE MILLION FOLLOWERS ...IN TARGET!

Written By **JEREMY BARTON**

Congratulation on purchase this book and thank You for doing so.

Please enjoy!

© Copyright 2019 by **JEREMY BARTON**

All rights reserved

This document is geared towards providing exact and reliable information with regards to the topic and issue covered. The publication is sold with the idea that the publisher is not required to render accounting, officially permitted, or otherwise, qualified services. If advice is necessary, legal or professional, a practiced individual in the profession should be ordered.

From a Declaration of Principles which was accepted and approved equally by a Committee of the American Bar Association and a Committee of Publishers and Associations.

In no way is it legal to reproduce, duplicate, or transmit any part of this document in either electronic means or printed format. Recording of this publication is strictly prohibited, and any storage of this document is not allowed unless with written permission from the publisher. All rights reserved.

The information provided herein is stated to be truthful and consistent, in that any liability, in terms of inattention or otherwise, by any usage or abuse of any policies, processes, or directions contained within is the solitary and utter responsibility of the recipient reader. Under no circumstances will any legal responsibility or blame be held against the publisher for any reparation, damages, or monetary loss due to the information herein, either directly or indirectly.

Respective authors own all copyrights not held by the publisher.

The information herein is offered for informational purposes solely and is universal as so. The presentation of the information is without a contract or any guarantee assurance.

The trademarks that are used are without any consent, and the publication of the trademark is without permission or backing by the trademark owner. All trademarks and brands within this book are for clarifying purposes only and are owned by the owners themselves, not affiliated with this document.

PRINTED IN USA

PREMISE

One of the greatest problems I see in Instagram marketing is the overload of information. People try to consume too many contents from different sources, which leads to inactivity and confusion. Experts are no different than newborns. The idea of success on Instagram is starting to seem like a big waste of time. You get discouraged, indulge and go back to your old ways of marketing. I want you to believe the information in this book. It's not a theoretical framework I imagined sounds good on paper. You have information that I personally used to achieve tremendous success on many Instagram accounts in multiple niches.

This is the only thing you really need to get an idea of if you want to achieve quick and long-term success on this desired social media platform: Instagram marketers do what 99.9% of users will not do. Don't treat it as something that can be rushed together and updated without worry or attention. Each element is designed with care and determination to achieve its goal: improve and increase traffic, increase commitment, increase sales through higher conversion rates.

Even if you use all the tips in this book to prepare for mass growth, you will only use one or two tips to improve your success on Instagram. If you are a beginner on Instagram, you can follow everything in chronological order. Experienced veterans will see in this book a reminder of what they already know, combined with new ideas that can help them break the longstanding growth chart that many Instagram influencers go through.

If you are a business: This book explains exactly how to grow your Instagram account quickly, attract significant traffic to your website or sales funnel, and how to gather certain emails faster than any other website. If you are not a business, the you should get ready to discover how your Instagram page can become a business and make money, regardless of your previous experience! I hope you are ready to generate predictable earnings and tremendous growth and dedication on your Instagram page.

Let's dive in!

TABLE OF CONTENTS

THE INSTAGRAM ENVIRONMENT ------------------------1

THE HASHTAGS ---29

DAILY ROUTINES TO BOOST ENGAGEMENT.------46

SHOUTOUTS & INSTAGRAM INFLUENCERS ---------54

CONNECTING WITH INSTAGRAM INFLUENCERS 67

HOW TO BUILD YOUR BRAND -----------------------------70

HOW TO USE INSTAGRAM VIDEOS FOR BUSINESS ----108

HOW TO USE INSTAGRAM STORIES FOR BUSINESS ---123

INSTAGRAM INFLUENCER----------------------------------130

HOW TO UTILIZE INSTAGRAM WITH YOUR DIRECT SALES BUSINESS ---156

INFLUENCER MARKETING DEFINED?-----------------168

GUIDE TO CREATING INSTGRAM ADS----------------180

INFLUENCER MARKETING RESEARCH TOOLS---206

DECIDING YOUR PRICE AS AN INFLUENCER-----220

EARNING WITH INSTAGRAM SPONSORSHIP.------246

WAYS TO EARN MONEY USING INSTAGRAM------256

TOP INSTAGRAM INFLUENCERS -------------------------262

THE INSTAGRAM ENVIRONMENT

Before you quickly follow the tips, tricks, secrets and strategies in this book, you need to understand exactly what you are encountering with your Instagram environment. Otherwise you will burn a lot of time trying to learn strategies that will not give you the best results. You need to learn how Instagram works before you get started and use the tactics described in this book. Consider this as an introduction for those new to Instagram. Experts should read this as a brief reminder.

1. INSTAGRAM IS 99.9%

MOBILE The vast majority of Instagram users access the app through their mobile device. It's much easier to use on your phone than a desktop application, and it won't change in the near future. All you have to do is look and feel on your mobile device. Suppose what you see is what everyone sees. Be sure to show your settings and changes on the mobile app to see how they look. This is very different from any other application on social media where the commitment is evenly distributed across multiple platforms. This also applies to all sales copies you use on Instagram. With limited space, long sales letters have no place on Instagram. Why? Because there is much less space (and time) to convey your message.

Here's another way of looking: People are addicted to their phones and find it difficult to look down. Your subscribers and customers are hoping to use the content they like on Instagram. They scroll through and quickly scroll through all the articles in their news feed. Therefore, it is important to immediately grab their attention and offer them value when they see your Instagram article. You should worry about the fact that 0.1% of people use Instagram on desktops because almost everyone spends all their time on their phone. Recently, a Pew research study found that "nearly 80% of social media time is spent on a mobile device." On the second level, everything on your site or sales funnel, assuming you have one, must be fully optimized for mobile use. It is set up for easy viewing on your phone.

If your site is not mobile optimized, you are wasting money. The desktop version of Instagram is mainly used to control third-party applications and to change specific settings. Outside of these two functions does not serve much. In fact, the desktop version has only recently appeared. To date, you will always post your Instagram account from the desktop version (unless you are using one of the third-party risk apps). This may seem like a waste to you until you realize how incredibly easy it is to use Instagram on the go. This is what leads to the very active user base (over 650,000,000 monthly users) you see on this incredibly popular social media platform.

2. THE GAME IS HIGHLY VISUAL

Each photograph that you need to post must be of good quality, with no issue. Today, individuals expect at any rate clean and new pictures. As the standard is higher than at any other time, you may fall behind if you don't keep this basic guideline. People are, ordinarily, incredibly visual animals. We unravel visual data a lot quicker than some other sort of media and a large portion of the data handled by our minds is visual. Research has indicated that we recollect clear pictures far superior to whatever else. Instagram exploits this organic rule. Inside this guide, you will discover how to utilize special visualizations to your advantage. At the point when you apply the standards I educated for clear photographs, your site will turn into a gala for the eyes of all who see it and, subsequently, will draw in more followers. The end is clear: you have to make exceptionally visual substance. Your Instagram posts ought to be clean and all around considered. The individuals who figure they can simply contact arbitrary things and call them content are the ones who consume quicker and end bankrupt.

3. MASSIVE COMMUNITIES ARE ALREADY ON INSTAGRAM

Despite the fact that you will make your very own base, you should understand that there are now colossal gatherings of individuals that exist on Instagram inside for all intents and purposes each specialty. You have to pinpoint precisely where they are and make sense of how to take advantage of them. This is imperative to understand on the off chance that you need to drive massive traffic to your Instagram page and grow your devotee base very quick. This all doesn't appear to be excessively mind boggling, isn't that right? That is the way ludicrously basic the Instagram platform is. Notwithstanding, you have to apply laser center in following and executing the systems in this book with a total understanding of the Instagram condition before you can viably exploit the massive communities and use them to drive traffic, grow your very own devotee base and at last produce reliable and unsurprising benefits. Since you comprehend what's in store on this astonishing platform, you are prepared to start setting up your Instagram profile.

Steps to Creating a Perfect Instagram

If you as of now have an Instagram account you can skim through these initial scarcely any passages however make certain to carefully peruse the following area when I talk about picking your Instagram name. Setting up an Instagram account is extremely easy and should take you close to several seconds. Download the application to your cell phone and open it up. On the principle screen, you will have the choice to sign in with your Facebook login or utilize your email address. Choose one and proceed onward. You will have the option to build out your profile with the accompanying subtleties:

• Your Full name: This is the name of your image/business (or your own name) explained in full (ex. Lift Your Mindset)

• Username: After rounding out the abovementioned, you will get a programmed proposal for what your username ought to be. This is independent from your full name discussed above (ex. @ElevateYourMindset)

• Password: Be sure that you choose something that is secure and easy to recollect Photo: Use your logo or an image of yourself if it's an individual page

Click on "Done", and you will quickly approach the Instagram platform and your new Instagram account. Try not to stress over getting everything immaculate immediately. As you study and read through this book, you will learn precisely how to build your existing account or new into a powerhouse brand and start drawing in new followers easily. This is basically the initial process.

NAME: WHAT PEOPLE WILL KNOW YOUR INSTAGRAM PAGE AS

The name you select for your Instagram page is absolutely crucial. Your Instagram name is similar to the domain name of a modern website these days. When people are looking for you, it must be recognizable and appear immediately. Your way of putting together a name will determine an important part of your success on Instagram. Unless it is a world-famous brand or celebrity that everyone knows by name, people should read their name and have a good idea of what their brand represents. This is the first step towards maximizing your growth on Instagram. People will be disappointed or confused if they see content that doesn't fit their name. Everything: Promotions, Ads, etc. - Will produce bad results if you make a mistake. Does that sound like common sense? That is for sure, until you realize how many people will get triggered in the process and won't be able to grow and take advantage of Instagram even before you begin. Don't rush this! You don't have to be a perfectionist, but you want to take the time to find the right name. Ask your friends, family, who you trust. You look for their brutally honest first impression when they see and hear your name.

Here are two or three things to keep an eye out for when you're picking your Instagram name:

Articulation: It ought to be anything but difficult to state your name. No part of your name ought to befuddle by any means.

Unique: Obviously, you can't utilize a username that has just been taken. You likewise need to maintain a strategic distance from likenesses to some other organizations or brands that are as of now on Instagram. Copyright encroachment issues will return to haunt you when you start developing your page sooner rather than later.

Periods as well as Underscores: You may need to utilize these so as to make a unique name for yourself. In a perfect world you need to abstain from utilizing them at everything except this probably won't be sensible. Point of confinement your utilization of these, and never put at least two periods/underscores directly adjacent to each other. The purpose behind this is on the grounds that it makes it difficult for people to search for you and find your name. Google will see "word1.word2.word3.word4" as four separate words, making the revelation of your page considerably more troublesome.

Length: This ought not be excessively long (the equivalent goes for your Full Name). To what extent? Go to any page and take a look at who they are following. The full name AND the username ought not be cut off by any means. This does is add equivocalness and perplexity to potential devotees who don't comprehend what your page is about. Compactness and clarity are critical to an effective Instagram name – this is the reason you should take as much time as necessary. Shorter names are not difficult to search for and may furnish you with restrictiveness.

Sexual orientation/Ethnicity/Religion: Keep these out of your name. Except if that is your particular niche, you are going as far as possible the potential size of your group of spectators before you even start. You need to regard what your supporters need to check whether you need to keep them around and connected with your content and Instagram page.

Prominent Names: Try to keep these out of your name (ex. Achievement, business visionary, very rich person, and so forth.). There are a few colossal Instagram accounts that command in these niches and you will confront a lofty tough move as you endeavor to develop your following. A unique name will make your page a lot easier to find when people are searching for you.

Importance: As expressed prior, you need your name to be applicable to the content you post. Utilize your niche's catchphrase in the initial segment of your name and not the center or last part of it. Enter the brain of an individual who is searching for your niche: What is the

FIRST thing they will type in the search field on the Instagram application? The watchword. On the off chance that your pledge isn't there, it will get lost among the other search results. This is a straightforward method to use search motor enhancement inside the Instagram condition.

Like your site: If you as of now have a website, have a go at setting up a domain that is or is fundamentally the same as your picked Instagram username. You need to go through a lot of cash for this, and you can even have an email address that incorporates your Instagram username. In view of individual experience, contact@username.com gives the most clarity since people know precisely who they are conversing with when sending messages. This email likewise offers unrivaled outcomes for something like a Gmail address, regardless of whether a username is remembered for this Gmail account (e.g., username @ gmail.com). Be that as it may, Gmail is the best choice in the event that you don't at present have a safe website or domain name.

Furthermore, if enough people click on your site, which will be featured in your profile – (more on that later), you will at last achieve a higher request rank on Google and you will find that people can find you outside of the Instagram arrange. You don't generally need to focus a lot on this anyway as you create you may find it beneficial. As extraordinary as Instagram is by all accounts, an overall brand is worked off of numerous stages through which will help you with ending up being undeniably logically accessible to people far and wide.

Verified Across Multiple Platforms: This is progressively significant towards those that need to extend their span on multiple internet based life platforms (Facebook, Twitter, Snapchat, YouTube, and so forth). This guarantees your marking is improved and bound together. The main exemption to this is you need to keep your personal records separate from the records you use for organizations and impacting. Except if your model expects you to be an indispensable piece of the page, you will lose adherents if people see steady selfies of yourself and not the substance that they need and hope to get.

Before you select your last Instagram username, you need to be clear about what you are building. Is it true that you are building your very own page, something for your business, or a general page on Instagram that spotlights on a particular specialty? This will influence the name you pick and you may even need to revisit the past criterias I spread out to guarantee that your Instagram name breezes through every one of the assessments.

THE 3 MOST COMMON KIND OF INSTAGRAM ACCOUNT.

Personal: A personal account is the one where people share features and energizing moments from their personal lives. Here, you can set up a convincing name that concentrates around you (or your brand) and your life. For instance, Gary Vaynerchuk has the username @garyvee. It's what he calls himself and everybody knows precisely who it is the point at which they hear this epithet. You need that equivalent sort of 'moment' acknowledgment for yourself.

Business: A business page as a rule posts items and administrations for people to find with expectations of obtaining another client or client. In this specific circumstance, your name should be alluring to your niche thus it must adhere to the above rules so as to pull in your optimal client or client to your Instagram page. Simultaneously, you additionally need something that promptly brings your very own brand into light. Concentrate on the advantages of working with your brand and not really the brand in general. This implies you need to maintain a strategic distance from CO's, INC's, or LLC's in your name.

Niche Page: Also known as the energy page. The key here is to fabricate a conspicuous name that people can connect with your brand and your brand as it were. You need your name to envelop your niche AND give an advantage or a significance. People need to peruse your name and promptly recognize what you do. This is essential for getting more supporters to your Instagram page rapidly – alongside after some time also. Presently, I need to advise you that on the off chance that you have plans to adapt your Instagram page, you have to pick a name that is as of now connected with a gainful niche. There's no reason for making your very own market when you can take advantage of ones that are as of now created through long periods of difficult work. Turning into a pioneer on Instagram isn't the most ideal approach to quicken your benefits, model what works and don't endeavor to waste time.

Here is a little example of the niches on Instagram that I know as a matter of fact are incredible in impact and size. In the event that your niche isn't recorded beneath, you should do some research to check whether it is practical for you to benefit from the niche you choose:

Religion;

Health;

Fitness/Nutrition;

Finance;

Beauty;

Development;

Motivation/Inspiration;

Success/Personal;

Real Estate;

Business/Entrepreneurship;

Travel Lifestyle (ex. high-end luxury);

Pets.

Each niche will have its advantages and disadvantages. You have to choose the one that works best for you. Ready to use your niche long enough to succeed and make money on Instagram, even if it takes a lot of work? Even if you are planning to make money on Instagram, choosing a niche with a large audience is key if you want to accelerate your growth and influence on Instagram.

Your Instagram Logo

The first and important thing anyone will notice when they visit a page on Instagram will not be its content, it will be their logo. Your logo is an image of your profile that represents you and your brand. You have the opportunity and the opportunity to impress with your logo the person who visits your Instagram page. If you don't seduce people with very visual images on your profile, you have to create a visual connection and that starts with your logo. One of the basics taught about Instagram is that it has to be mobile. What exactly does this mean?

This means that people will not see an enlarged photo of their logo unless they go directly to their page. It will actually look a lot less when people are browsing through their news and watching it. In this small visual space, you need to get someone's attention in less than a second. Once you start creating an audience and creating loyal subscribers, your logo becomes an integral part of your brand identity. For example, when your publication appears in the news about your subscribers, a powerful logo can attract powerful attention. Recognizing it can mean the difference between stopping users and interacting with your Instagram post or just scrolling.

Also, when you start commenting on other people's posts, responding to comments in your own post, or like other people's comments, your logo will appear as a notification on the user's account. Instagram. Those little contact points your brand has with these customers are the key to interacting with other accounts and their subscribers. A powerful logo that stands out in your announcements or news is key to getting your attention and putting your brand in the forefront. Here are two simple steps you can take to create a powerful logo for your Instagram page:

BE BOLD: Your logo should stand out! It will occupy the upper left corner of every message you write. To do this, you can use a white or dark background and then display the logo in contrast, using a different color scheme. Finally, your brand will be built and recognized based on its name, logo and content. Your logo should get the attention of others if you want your brand to be recognized. When people first visit your site, you want your logo to be clear and concise. This could mean the difference between leaving your site immediately or becoming a loyal follower. Do you know how to talk about Apple? When you see the Apple Store, you might even need the name "Apple". All you need is a quick recognition of your brand symbols and you know who it is right away. You also know exactly what they are preparing. The type of instant and quick recognition you want to get with your logo. You want your name and content to spread beyond the platform of Instagram. People should discover and look at your logo and recognize it, as well as your brand, in no time.

Keep it simple: I like the quote that says, "The last form of sophistication is simplicity. Perfection is not when you can't add anything, but when you can't take anything away. Look at the biggest and most influential Instagram pages, both globally and in your niche. You will notice that his logo is NOT complex, instead of simple and accurate. You don't have to imagine or worry about complex details. Instagram users won't be able to see small details on their mobile phones, and if they are too complex, they will have trouble associating the logo with their brand. you see the Nike check mark symbol, you should think about what it is. You know precisely what it means and you recognize it when you see it. You want people to think about your logo and what it represents.

Why Instagram Is So Powerful for Your Personal Brand and Business

Do you know how powerful Instagram is?

Most people have heard of an app called Instagram; It took the entire world by storm. It does not matter or make a difference if you are a technology savvy who knows the latest and greatest applications, or you can merly check your email. We can all agree that somebody we know is still on Instagram. If you look around today, it's rare that you don't see someone stuck in your phone, completely unaware of what's going on around you. It's really interesting to see how many individual use their phone in the middle of a conversation, sometimes more focused on their phone than in the conversation they have with the person in front of them. Has this ever occured to you or maybe you did it yourself?

We live in another world. unlike 10-20 years ago. At the time, smartphones were not that smart, apps we didn't have that often, and people weren't completely fascinated with their phones and, more importantly, the apps they use on them. Today, you can use apps like Instagram to talk to friends, either by tagging them in a message you saw, by sending them a video message, in response to a story they posted. or even see something that reminded you. You will be amazed and explore different cities, see your favorite actor every day of your life or your favorite comedian or some of the best moments of last night's game. None of this was in existence 15 years ago, at the time people could watch television for fun, but now people spend more time on their phone than ever, and it's on Instagram, which spends most of their time. Whether you have a business or maybe want to grow your own personal brand ... Instagram is definitely one of the platforms you need to use, here we explain why.

Are you aware that you have access to more than 800 million users every month on Instagram? Instagram is rapidly rising to the top of all social media platforms and with its 800 million users, it is without doubt one of the best platforms to reach your target audience. While there have been 350 million users on Twitter in recent years, Instagram has already exceeded this figure and will reach one billion users in a year or two. As the old saying goes: "Know your customers and people where they are." And now they're on Instagram, and Instagram is on your phone, which makes it even more cool and powerful. Take a look around, you can locate someone looking at your phone and, more importantly, utilizing Instagram.

Instagram makes Networking simpler for you. The networking capacities and broad reach that Instagram has given us, on a worldwide scale is unparalleled. Brilliant people such as yourself realize they should make the most of each chance to develop and grow their network. Instagram enables you to connect with people dependent on their inclinations, area, hash labels and shared companions and contacts. The good part is you can build your network all around the world from your cell phone. Presently, this really presents you a reasonable justification for all the time you spend on Instagram.

Instagram aids your reach and engagement. Instagram has 58 times more reach and supporter engagement than Facebook, and a bewildering 120 times more reach than Twitter. So building your Instagram audience is imperative to your advancement now and many more of it in the coming future. On the off chance that your not building your targeted audience (people who are keen on your business or personal brand) it's practically similar to not having a wireless or email for people to get in touch with you. It is similar a fisher men not having an angling rod post or net to catch fish, or a stylist without scissors to trim hair, we're certain you get the point at this point. Start growing your audience today so you can begin picking up momentum and introduction preparing you for the future with a strong foundation to build on.

Instagram is fun and easy to utilize. For the people who know about Instagram, you definitely realize how fun and easy it is to utilize. Regardless of whether you have a personal or a business account you likely as of now see how amazing and exciting Instagram can be. People can investigate various urban areas, nations, and landmasses directly from their telephone and furthermore observe and do live recordings for their audience. You can go along with somebody start a live video, talk with style. also, the conceivable outcomes are inestimable with new element being included frequently. Instagram allows you to basically own your on TV network without the TV network cost. Far and away superior you can get live input from your audience with remarks and engagement directly as you are interacting with them, that is more dominant than TV.

People love pictures now and consistently have and will continue to do that. For those individuals that have never utilized Instagram, it very well may be an astonishing method to connect with individuals and build a targeted audience that is profoundly engaged. You can build an audience that is neighborhood, across the country, or worldwide relying upon your inclination; brand, callings, or enthusiasm. There is a familiar axiom, " words generally can't do a picture justice." Start utilizing Instagram today, and allow your photos state a huge number of words for you. People have constantly adored pictures for ages so you know Instagram will be here for the long stretch.

Utilizing Instagram you can make important connections. A great deal of people know at this point Instagram has been developing significantly. Particularly over the most recent quite a long while, presently the planning is ideal for you. Everyone knows somebody that is consistently on their telephone checking their Instagram, and all the more significantly Instagram holds people's consideration. It has gotten one of the most aweome platforms that people and organizations can use to connect with others. Would you be able to envision connecting with new people and potential clients ordinary essentially from utilizing Instagram. Look at the possibility that you had the option to develop a rich, significant, connection with your audience. Simultaneously make and develop your own brand and nearness in the brains of people everywhere throughout the world. Also likewise to keep awake to date with loved ones, Instagram genuinely enables you to do everything and the sky will be the starting place from that point.

It is imperative to grow your audience on Instagram, but growing your Instagram yourself is hard with the ever changing algorithm. It makes it even hard for you to grow your account. You can likewise post daily content and you might not be experiencing the type of growth you expected.

Much the same as other social platforms and systems, Instagram can be utilized to build and grow your brand for your business when utilized justified and keen way. Instagram fills in as a device of making your business accessible and open to the purchasers. Online networking promoting using Instagram can open up a universe of chance for your brand. It is in this way clear Instagram is significant for your business. The inquiry comes from about how you can build your business with Instagram and beneath is the response to that question.

To start with, you have to direct a research to know the best businesses on Instagram. You additionally need to look at different brands in the business and furthermore know who your rivals are with the goal that you can comprehend what methodologies to use so as to build your business. You should constantly set sensible Instagram objectives that bind back to your business objectives. These objectives ought to incorporate expanding awareness with hashtag focusing on. Expanding item mindfulness and expanding traffic to your website. You should then concoct a procedure of posting your content. Here you have to ponder about how frequently you post, what time to post, and choosing your content subjects. You have to maintaining a standard posting while simultaneously stay away from an excessive amount of posting.

Recall that Instagram is about visuals. Your profile photograph ought to be your company's logo. You have to pick one filter that you will use for most of your photos. By selecting one filter for your photos it makes your brand simple to perceived. your photos easier for your followers. Guarantee to post photos that reflects the character and culture of your business. In the event that you don't know on the most proficient method to outwardly speak to your company, you ought to consider observing the records of your followers so as to recognize what they are re sharing. This will enable you to know their patterns and consequently help you to proficiently introduce your business.

Another strategy that you can use to build your business on Instagram is the branded hashtag. You should find a hashtag that typifies your Instagram brand and urge your followers to share photos that fit that picture. This will enable your brands to be presented to new potential clients and this is an opportunity for your business to grow. You ought to likewise consider geotagging. This is adding your area to your photos when you post them. It is exceptionally successful as it makes your followers realize where to find you and your business. All the more along these lines, followers who live close to you will love to cooperate with you and your business. You should likewise post restrictive positions on your Instagram. This should be possible through offering limits to your followers, it will make them feel exceptional and subsequently inform others regarding your business. Instagram can really be utilized to build your business, attempt it today and appreciate the advantages.

HOW TO CRAFT A BIO/PROFILE THAT GENERATES BUYERS

When people see your attractive logo and username, they will quickly look at their bio / profile. Your profile is on your Instagram page just below your logo. Now is enough time to make a good impression. You only have a few lines and that's it. A copy of a long-form sale has no place in your bio / profile and will attract more followers than you will attract. There is a systematic way I chose to create my biography profile. You can utilize a template as a general guide and try different versions of your Instagram profile until everything is right. One of the benefits of Instagram is the speed at which you can try out ideas and get comments whether they work or not. We cover some elements that are part of your bio / Instagram profile:

Bullets: You want your profile to contain bullets and your sentences should be in one line. Your profile should be quite easy to read and focused on. Play around with pens to get those that look clean and professional.

Summary: Since you only focus on one line at a time, you have no choice but to keep things simple. It makes your job easier and allows people to read your Instagram profile easily. This way, there is no confusion between your Instagram page and its existence.

In summation, your bio/profile on Instagram ought to be spotless and sorted out with content that people can retain effectively and rapidly. Directly underneath your logo will be your profile name, which is independent from your genuine page name. You can essentially decide to re-express your page name except if you have something explicit that you are centered around (ex. "Helping Entrepreneurs Succeed"). Hanging in the balance underneath that, you can have a showcasing message in the event that it is reliably utilized over your advertising. For example, if I was Nike, I can consider using "Take care of business" in this line. When your profile name and tagline are flawless, you're prepared to proceed onward profoundly of your Instagram profile. Every single line here checks, so give close consideration!

Your first line should be about your WHY – why you made your brand. You need to generate curiosity and enthusiasm for the potential devotees that are visiting your page. This talks directly to who I need to pull in as my center adherent base. It additionally makes a feeling of network in light of the fact that the potential supporter may feel included in the event that they accept they have a raised attitude. This is imperative and you need to find something about your brand's 'the reason' that people can identify with and feel separated of.

Next, you need to concentrate on your WHAT. Would could it be that you are doing? Would could it be that you need people to do? In the event that you are advancing a product, you ought to be direct and forthright about it. "Look at my most recent certainty course" is direct and you are creating curiosity about this course in a straightforward manner. Your Instagram profile is an extraordinary spot to drive people to the link where your product is found (in the event that it as of now has a site set available). You can without much of a stretch MONETIZE your product or administration along these lines!

At long last, the manner in which you post the link in your bio/profile is significant. People need to see your link and realize that they are getting precisely what is promoted in your bio. If you have a product about certainty, the word 'certainty' ought to show up some place in the URL of your link. This implies in the event that you are utilizing a link shortening administration like Bit.ly you have to put your product name in that URL. Try not to put something like: bit.ly/2lrKZn5b. People will believe it's a trick and they won't tap on it.

Additionally, if that you can, leave the "www" out and underwrite the main letter of the word for the sake of your link "NameOfWebsite.com." I've discovered that I have the most noteworthy number of snaps when links were streamlined and illuminated with the principal letter promoted along these lines. You generate curiosity, you set up your motivation, you direct them to your link through your source of inspiration so they can become familiar with that charming thing in your bio. On the off chance that your business funnel is arrangement appropriately, it will deal with the rest.

Here are a few great tips that you should follow when creating your profile/bio:

MAXIMUM of 4-LINE

Except if you completely need to, keep your bio to four lines or less. What's more, consistently make sure the product in the link is consistent with your whoops and promotions. Ifyou have a link in your bio, it MUST match up with the url link of the product or the business that you are promoting. Promoting a video course just to drive people to a digital book will execute your traffic stream. People definitely comprehend what they need before they visit your website and breaking that desire will hurt your brand and radically diminish your changes.

Besides, your profile/bio must be consistent with your promotion. Congruency in this Instagram-style sales funnel is critical! People don't have the opportunity or the capacity to focus to attempt to make sense of what you are promoting and they will essentially proceed onward to the following page on the off chance that you need coinciding. The design in your website or sales funnel and the promotion needs to be in phase. When you have your advertisement/whoop prepared, you have to make sure that the design in your promotion AND showcasing message are consistent. The informing (for example your duplicate) and the shading plan need to match. I have seen my best change rates when I've kept these two things consistent in the promotion, bio AND website/sales funnel.

This implies your website or sales funnel, if that is your showcasing vessel, should be exceptionally visual (you'll become familiar with much increasingly about this all through this book). People are familiar with great design and are very killed by poor visuals, particularly coming directly from Instagram which is loaded up with profoundly visual substance. An absence of perfect and fresh visuals will prompt low transformations. In the event that your target on Instagram is to get people to select in to your presentation page or purchase your products and administrations you will be amazingly frustrated in your outcomes in the event that you design your webpages with low quality or potentially pixelated pictures.

YOUR CONTACT INFORMATION ON YOUR PROFILE / BIO FUND

Giving your subscribers a way to contact you directly is a great way to build long-term relationships and make SALES. If you would like to be reahed by email, please provide your email if you would like to be contacted by DM, please notify your subscribers. Many influential Instagram people like to communicate via the free KIK app, which may also be an option for you. Simply explain how people who visit your Instagram page can contact you.

THE HASHTAGS

The Hashtag Lie

This is the part that you were probably wondering about. With so many people using hashtags all the time on Instagram, they must be super important. Right?

Wrong! There's actually a hard limit on the amount of hashtags that you should be using. And just because you can post up to 30 hashtags on a picture does not mean that you should. Here is what happens if you go down this route: Sure, you'll get lots of new followers and an increased amount of likes. You must be getting greater engagement. Not so fast! For one, you are going to attract automation bots that are specifically programmed to like or follow people who post using a certain hashtag. This dilutes your following of engaged followers and decreases your engagement rate over the long-term which annihilates your chances of consistently making it to the Explore page on Instagram. Additionally, you are attracting people that might not see your posts or page, let alone be interested in the niche that you cater to.

In short, using excessive hashtags is just a game of improving your likes and followers for the sake of having higher numbers. If you recall from earlier discussions in this book, you know that more followers does not necessarily means to more dollars in your bank account. The primary focus of this entire book is to walk you through step-by-step how to generate predictable profits from your Instagram page. And in order to do that successfully you have to create a community of real and engaged followers that genuinely want your content. You cannot develop a loyal follower base by pasting 30 hashtags on each of your Instagram posts.

On the occasion that they are used, they are either specific to the post or their overall brand. The maximum number of hashtags you will see on large Instagram Influencer pages is 5, with 1 to 3 being the norm. Since hashtags lead to engagement from people who don't even see the post, you cannot know when you are receiving true engagement. This is why you should strive to leave any hashtags off of your content when you are testing new and different content strategies. Leave the game of hashtag oversaturation to people who don't understand the concept of acquiring real and engaged followers. Go the opposite direction and get real engagement that you can utilize to accurately track your growth. With that said, there is no need to completely demonize hashtags. Used sparingly and strategically, they can be yet another useful tool in your arsenal for increasing your follower base and your engagement.

Here are some strategies for using hashtags on your Instagram page effectively.

BE SPECIFIC

The most successful Instagram Influencers only use targeted hashtags or ones specific to their brand. You want to model that same approach. Using generic and spam hashtags (anything with a '4' in it) will hurt engagement in the long run because you will be unfollowed for not engaging back through commenting or following them. Plus, your followers aren't going to your page so that they can be spammed with endless hashtags in each photo. It looks out of place and some of your followers will get the impression that you are a bot-run spam page.

KEEP HASHTAGS INTHE COMMENTS

This ensures that your picture will be found when a particular hashtag is entered into the search field. It will allow your content more accessible to those who are searching for your hashtag but are not following you. Moreover, your caption is for valuable sales copy that gets people to take action (follow someone, click on the link in the bio, etc.). Don't take up valuable space with distracting hashtags. You can fix this by putting the hashtags in as a comment on the post. Just because this is so important I want to repeat this point and make it crystal clear: DO NOT put hashtags in the caption section of your Instagram post. Put your hashtags in as a comment on your Instagram post.

ROTATE BETWEENSETS OF HASHTAGS

Let's say that you have a number of hashtags that have worked well for you, but you know that spamming your content repeatedly with them won't help. Within your niche, you can have a set of hashtags that you sparingly use for specific scenarios. You can have a set of hashtags for posts about your personal life, another set of hashtags for inspirational posts, and perhaps a set of hashtags for your ad shoutouts. This helps you tap into audiences based on search results and you can bring in more engagement to your page. Ninja Hack: Have your hashtags saved in the notes section of your smartphone so all you have to do is just copy and paste them into the comments section of your Instagram post.

DO SOME HASHTAG RESEARCH

Of course, all of the tips above are predicated on doing your due diligence in finding the right hashtags to use. A great tool to use is: SocialRank.com. It's free of charge and allows you to research the key hashtags being used by your successful competitors. You can also find the users that identify most with key terms and the most frequently used hashtags within each of those terms. There are other things you can do with Social Rank, but it really stands out as a great hashtag research tool. Another great place to learn how to expand on your hashtags is: Hashtagify.me. Visit this website and learn how you can reach a broader audience on Instagram by finding hashtags that are close and similar to the ones you are currently using.

GEOTAG YOUR PHOTOS

This is a strategy I have not personally tested, but there are Instagram Influencers who swear that they have seen increased engagement on their posts from using geotags. Try it for yourself and maybe it will works for you. Here, you are geotagging your Instagram photos as a way to add locality to your Instagram posts. I can see where this would be especially useful if you are a local business looking for exposure in your city or town, or operating in a niche involving multiple locations around the world. It turns out that more and more Instagram users are using "Places -> Near Current Location" in the search function. If your post is geotagged and they are searching for something in your niche, you have opened up the door to gain local organic traffic.

In conclusion, hashtags can definitely help you grow your Instagram following as well as act as a navigational tool for helping people find your content. Used correctly and sparingly hashtags will spread your content throughout the Instagram platform. Consider them to be like an icing on the cake – they are nice to have but your business or brand will not fail because you forgot to use hashtags or you use the incorrect ones. Make sure you have the basic down pat before you start testing out different hashtag strategies.

Instagram can be profoundly successful, however you must be savvy about how you utilize it. That is the condition Instagram hashtags work so well.

Hashtags assist you with overseeing and search for proper substance on Instagram. They make it easy and straightforward for your intended interest group to find you and add enthusiasm to your offers. One Instagram study indicated that adding at any rate one hashtag to the entirety of your Instagram posts will, all things considered, generate over 12% greater engagement.

Grow and Extend Your Reach.

The extraordinary things on hashtags is their ability to get to a wide scope of people that may have literally nothing to do with your post and don't explicitly tail you on Instagram.

How Do Instagram Hashtags Work?

Suppose a client looks for the term 'gardening'. Instagram will show all the most recent posts that contain the 'gardening' keyword. By utilizing #gardening as your hashtag on a post, you are tell Instagram to put ahead your post any time time somebody searches for that term.

Hashtag the entirety of your posts with related keywords. Use words and terms you think Instagram sers will look for. Continuously use the # image before the word, utilize no accentuation, keep it as short as could be expected under the circumstances and use letters and numbers.

The Best Hashtags For Instagram

Stuffing indiscriminate hashtags all over Instagram won't work the magic for you. You'll need to plann and deliberately select the best and most well known hashtags to reach to the correct audience for your business. They ought to be fitting to the keywords looked by your target audience and you'll have to watch out for which ones perform best for you.

It will require some investment to find the best hashtags to utilize. A few procedures include:

• Check out the hashtags your rivals use all the time to showcase their business.

• Test different hashtags and assess your outcomes.

• Use an application for hashtag thoughts (like TagOMatic).

Making The Best out of Trending Hashtags

When an event happens, a hashtag is often created. If you can relate your message to the hashtag, those who follow the news will be more likely to see it.

It is crucial to control when a hashtag seems to be popular and publish content using this hashtag to take advantage of the large number of viewers it has received.

Look for other hashtags comparable to your page in the Instagram search engine. Use these hashtags when posting new content. This is another way to contact Instagram users who are still on the site but who are not following their messages.

Tips, Examples, and Explanations on How to utilize Hashtags effectively for your Business

Provided that you are new to internet based life you may considering what hashtags are about. We see them all over - Twitter, Facebook, Instagram, Google+, Pinterest and even Tumblr.

Be that as it may, what are they expected to do? For what reason do they appear to be so irregular? Who should utilize them?

It's no big surprise this all can appear to be extremely befuddling!

That is the reason I've assembled a few hints to enable you to comprehend what the hell hashtags are and how to utilize them deliberately in your business.

What are #Hashtags

Essentially hashtags help individuals discover stuff and offer stuff. They resemble an authoritative apparatus for online life. They are an approach to make it simpler for individuals to discover posts on a given point as long as those posts utilize the equivalent hashtag that is being looked for.

Hashtags are the place given words are introduced with the console pound hashtag sign: #. At least one words can be utilized if the hashtag and keyword(s) have no spaces in the middle of them. Once added to a web based life post, the hashtag expression winds up accessible and interactive.

For a model M&Ms just released another Pumpkin Spice enhanced sweet for Fall. Starbucks is likewise advancing their Pumpkin Spice latte. In the event that you go into Twitter and types hashtag PumkinSpice in the pursuit include, it will draw up a rundown of these and other Pumpkin Spice related posts.

Why Use #Hashtags

At the point when done appropriately and deliberately, hashtags are an incredible method to acquire introduction for your business. Here are a couple of models how:

Knowing prevalent hashtags for your industry and adding them to your posts can enable you to get traffic to your blog or site.

Looking hashtags encourages you do examine on points, keep an eye on your opposition, and find incredible substance.

Including hashtags can help brand yourself, your business, your items, and increase you acknowledgment.

Advancing explicit hashtags for a live occasion can pick up network among your participants and devotees.

 What's more, a few people use hashtags for no reason in particular or to come to a meaningful conclusion. My most loved is #ChocolateIsSacred and have utilized it more than once!

Peruse more beneath about key approaches to utilize hashtags in your business.

When Hashtags Were First Created

Twitter made the #hashtag include on June 1, 2009. All Twitter hashtags (words with the # sign before them) progressed toward becoming hyperlinks to find more tweets relating to that subject.

Other interpersonal organizations before long pursued, for example, Facebook in 2013, Pinterest, Google+, Tumblr, and Instagram. A few systems like Google+ and Instagram have grasped hashtags with a rage where Facebook still slacks at bringing this component into standard utilization.

Actually, quite recently I led an exceptionally casual overview about the utilization of hashtags on Facebook and many said they had no clue what they were, others thought they were malicious and jumbled up their newsfeed and most all never tapped on them. For sure, the main individuals who were utilizing hashtags were either advertisers or web based life chiefs!
In any case, that doesn't mean they shouldn't be utilized... as you'll see there are a lot of motivations to fuse them into your web based life system.

Principles for Hashtag Use

Various stages have diverse official and "unwritten" runs about utilizing hashtags. Here's a couple to know about:

Sentence case doesn't make a difference, yet you can utilize it to improve intelligibility like: #SecretStarbucksMenu.

You can't utilize exceptional characters, for example, runs, indicators and so on.

Try not to get malicious. Three or less hashtags is immaculate. Utilize such a large number of and it very well may be considered hashtag spam.

Abstain from having your Twitter or Instagram presents naturally send on Facebook when you will in general utilize a great deal of hashtags. This is a genuine mood killer for those on Facebook.

Research a hashtag before utilizing it. A current hashtag might be utilized for something different that you would prefer not to be related with or cause to notice.

Hashtags: Strategic Examples On To Use It Effectively For Your Business

Much the same as knowing the best catchphrases of your industry and upgrading your site substance to incorporate them so as to bc found in web search tools, hashtags can likewise be utilized to enable you to get found in internet based life.

It's critical to make Hashtags for:

Occasions you are holding. For instance the Pacific National Exposition in Vancouver simply finished for one more year and all through their Twitter campaigns, they utilized #TheFair hashtag as found in this model beneath.

Labeling well known individuals or huge organizations who are referenced in a post. For example, hastag Elvis Presely brings about several posts about the King of Rock and Roll.

Presents related on slanting themes. Creator and Spiritual Teacher Wayne Dyer as of late passed away. The hashtag RIP WayneDyer was made to take advantage of the social scans for news identifying with his passing.

Doing research. For instance, in the event that you were doing research on the most recent news for our up and coming Canadian Federal political race, do a Hashtag search utilizing # CanadianElection2015to discover a few posts regarding the matter.

Item advancement. Making an uncommon hashtag for your image or item can enable you to increase a fan base. Making a hashtag for your book or motion picture can help get footing and transform it into an inclining theme.

Funniness. Individuals likewise use hashtags as an approach to impart amusing stuff to other people and have a decent snicker. Here's a hashtag utilized by late night anchor person Jimmy Fallon depicting his companion's vehicle and going on an excursion with him.

Well known Industry Topics. In the event that you see a post on a well known industry point, by adding that equivalent hashtag to a post you make will enable you to be found by others searching for substance on that hashtag.

Campaigns. Lots of individuals "screen" certain hashtags. So utilizing a hashtag reliably can enable you to increase an after. For instance Nike held a progression of advancements utilizing the #nikezoom hashtag.

Live Chats. Talks offer organizations the capacity to interface with their clients, broaden their scope and mindfulness. Be aware that making a hashtag can enable you to draw in individuals to visit. For Example #BeTheOne is a month to month visit about moving individuals to have any kind of effect through close to home authority that imbues uprightness, nobility and character.

Tap into Trending subjects. Counting a drifting hashtag in your post can build the general reach. Ritetag is an extraordinary instrument to help distinguish inclining hashtags to utilize. It enables you to look through 11 million hashtags to perceive what's hot or not, has a long life, is abused, and underused. That way you can choose the best hashtags to contact your group of spectators.

Organization or Personal Name. Addition acknowledgment by making an organization label like #Apple and #stephenking.

Statements. On the off chance that you offer statements, hashtags will enable you to be found. Some main ones to utilize are #motivationalquotes #inspirationalquotes and #quotes. Take a gander at the utilization of hashtags in one of our ongoing Twitter posts. Each subject identifying with the statement has its own hashtag.

Repeating post topics. For instance you may post a #photooftheday, #followfriday or #throwbackthursday for day by day or week by week repeating posts. We use #eTip as a day by day topic where we offer tips on different subjects business people use in their business.

Picking up blog perusers. Utilizing a hashtag on Pinterest pins can drive perusers back to your site or blog. At the point when somebody taps on a hashtag of yours the majority of the outcomes that are appeared on Pinterest connection back to related blog content. Note that these outcomes are fairly not quite the same as what you would discover in Twitter. Where Twitter presentations brings about sequential request, Pinterest shows in fame.

Research your rivals. Pursue hashtags your rivals use to do statistical surveying and keep up on their most recent news.

Hashtags are a ton of fun once you get the hang of it you'll be hashtagging as well as anyone.

Many photographers will gain from reading some or all of the sections as there is some overlap. Sometimes the searchable hashtags proposed under each section might seem glaringly obvious—you shoot documentary, do you really need to tell people that? Due to the nature of algorithms, the answer is often yes. There are two types of hashtag, searchable and submittable. Let's review the distinction.

Searchable

Tagging your image with a searchable hashtag will allow others to find it by filtering what they see through the search bar. For instance, say you photograph a swimming pool and tag it #swimmingpool, people interested in that hashtag are more likely to find you via the search bar. You can utilize as many or as few hashtags as you wish, the idea is that they all correspond to what we see or feel when looking at the photograph, or the process that led to its creation.

Submittable

Tagging your image with a submittable hashtag means that you are effectually submitting your work to a feature page for consideration—using the hashtag #myfeatureshoot, for example, means your photograph will be one of many submissions that the Feature Shoot Instagram page can choose from to share with their followers, if the editors like what they see. While some feature pages, like #myfeatureshoot show work from many genres, many feature pages only feature images with a particular theme, genre or aesthetic—it is crucial that your image meets the requirements of the page in order to be eligible.

DAILY ROUTINES TO BOOST ENGAGEMENT.

Instagram has become one of the most popular social media platforms with over 800 million active users. Creators use Instagram for a different reasons, but all of us crave the same two things in specific. Likes and Comments. Likes aren't just about approving a post, they're about giving positive feedback and connecting with people you care about, too. Thus, so many people are obsessed with likes and comments.

You may be pondering: The better your content is, the more likes and remarks you get, isn't that so? Well…wrong. This is what I mean: eye-getting content issues. Yet, after Instagram changed it's calculation, there's been a recognizable decrease in the natural reach of posts. In the event that you don't make sure your posts get seen on the feed, making intriguing and valuable content is an exercise in futility and exertion. The advice? Lift engagement on your Instagram!

While there's nobody size-fits-all technique to build your perceivability on Instagram, there are some noteworthy every day schedules that can help you a lot as they give a feeling of structure and pay off over the long haul. So here's the rundown of day by day schedules that can assist you with boosting engagement on Instagram:

1. Post visual content normally

For what reason is Instagram so popular?Because it's about visual content!It's nothing unexpected that most people are outwardly arranged, and 90% of information transmitted to our cerebrum is visual. Pictures catch eye and cause feelings, so people can spend incalculable hours looking over their Instagram feeds.How would it be able to support you? Posting on Instagram can bring you engagement you need. What's more, the most ideal approach to snare your followers is to post visual content regularly.However, you don't need to overpost as your followers may believe you're spamming them. Besides, you can't stand to miss distributing as they may disregard you. Accordingly, the way to progress is to keep a parity. As indicated by Union Metrics, you should post anyplace between1 to 2 times per day.

2. Track and analyze your followers

First of all: Do you have a business profile or individual page on Instagram? On the off chance that you need to increase your engagement on Instagram, it's prescribed you change to an Instagram business profile as it gives you a chance to see more experiences and, hence, permits you become more acquainted with your followers better.When you change to a business profile however, you may see the natural reach of your posts declining. To handle this, you'll need to post a greater amount of your content when your followers are online.Once you get your profile changed to a business account, simply tap on the Stats symbol to open up a totally different universe of bits of knowledge into your account's performance.

Here, you can get significant information about your followers to understand what they may need and when they are online The more followers you can reach, the more chances you need to associate with them. In this way, use Instagram Insights every day to know your audience from start to finish.

Pro tip: if you don't rely on statistics, you can poll your followers with the help of Insta Stories. Just ask them when it's better to post and get their honest answers!

3. Interact with your followers

You need to increase engagement, however let's face it: do you give your followers what they want?They may need a few likes and remarks from you, as well. There's nobody directional approach to social media in the event that you need to attempt to make it enormous on Instagram.Make sure your followers realize you're tuning in and that you truly care about their remarks by communicating with them or in any event, loving their remarks. You ought to be keen on their content too — like/remark on their posts to draw their consideration and addition dedication.

Have you at any point found out about the boomerang impact? Your activities represent themselves, and when you show followers that you're really inspired by them, they will be keen on your content.Don't be voracious for likes.Pro tip: Don't perform in excess of 350 preferences for every hour in the event that you don't have any desire to be blocked. Instagram has its point of confinement to keep clients from spammers and computerized mass enjoying tools.

4. Try Ephemeral Content

Instagrammers long for authenticity, and showing off camera minutes is a demonstrated method to build trust and loyalty.If you have never had a go at posting transient content, the opportunity has already come and gone to consider it.First of all, the fleeting content otherwise known as Instagram Stories disappear inside 24 hours, so Instagrammers watch it all the more regularly all together not to miss something significant. In addition, utilizing vaporous content is an approach to abstain from flooding your principle feed and get more perspectives. While your posts may get covered in the feed, Insta stories appear in succession at the highest point of the feed, so it's easier to see new uploads.

There are various modes: type, photos and recordings, boomerang, superzoom, rewind, without hands, stop-movement. The most ideal approach to support engagement is to remain imaginative and make the most out of giving transient content. Consistently is another chance to convey what needs be on Instagram.

Expert tip: Steaming live recordings builds the quantity of people who visit your account as the majority of your followers get a warning when you go live.

5. Reach potential audience

Do you need more people to follow your account?Find your intended interest group and be interested in their content first!Moreover, reaching your potential audience naturally is an approach to grab their attention without putting resources into advertising. It's in our temperament to pay attention to people who are interested in us, so most Instagrammers check obscure accounts who like and remark on their posts. Furthermore, it assurances to give more people a chance to understand increasingly about you.If you have a monstrous following on Instagram, you can share your potential audience's photos and label them on your account to promote them and stand out for them too.

Truth be told, people give about 80% of every single social medium posts to discussing themselves, so people trust different clients who hear them out. Hence, being interested in your potential audience's content is a demonstrated method to get increasingly steadfast followers and, subsequently, better engagement.

Expert tip: follow your potential supporters and communicate with them now and again to grab their attention. For instance, I have a Google Drive record where I post links to remarks I've left on potential audience's profiles all together not to overlook them.

6. Maintain Long-Term Connections

If you accept that posting content on your account is sufficient to help engagement, I have some bad news for you. You have to build a following and furthermore keep up a long-term association with guarantee that your followers care about your content too.To build great association, you have to speak with your followers, and furthermore like and remark on their posts, label them in your photos, and watch their stories. Yet in addition remember to be pertinent in your posts — don't share nasty content as it harms trust level.Once you've discovered a fascinating post on Instagram, you can send it by means of direct message to encourage an increasingly authentic relationship.

Pro tip: slide into followers' DMs and offer something unique with them. People consistently esteem an individual approach.

7. Find Inspiration

If you need to distribute crisp and convincing content all the time, you have to remain innovative. With regards to inventiveness, motivation matters, and finding wellsprings of motivation is a key to success.To help imagination, follow fascinating accounts and attract motivation from them to get experiences. For instance, you can find masters in your niche and track their updates to perceive what they post to get a clue on what you can create to add to your feed.Now you don't need to save photos to your telephone or PC — tap on a bookmark symbol to sort out private assortments to save photos on Instagram.

While you can create private assortments, it's likewise easier to sort photos and find what you need quicker when your saved photos are grouped.

Genius tip: Turn on warnings if you've discovered somebody moving and you don't have any desire to miss their posts.

8. Keep an Eye on Trends

Having a social media nearness isn't sufficient to pull in new followers. You have to realize how to intrigue them, and watching out for patterns is an approach to understand what kind of content you should post to grab their attention. Actually, social media patterns have the most noteworthy potential of boosting engagement.For model, you can reach increasingly potential followers in the event that you add a geotag in stories as your story may appear on the prescribed feed. Additionally, you can save the most intriguing stories utilizing the stories features feature. This will enable your profile guests to see your top content in a separate area underneath your profile.

NB: you have to know Instagram patterns to understand what to post. For instance, video content is blasting on the web, yet photos get greater engagement on Instagram.

Instagram changes its calculations regularly, so you have to follow what is trendy day by day so as to not miss significant updates.

Professional tip: Bookmark and watch out for the Business Instagram blog as they share ongoing updates.

SHOUTOUTS & INSTAGRAM INFLUENCERS

For the vast majority of people, businesses and brands who begin using Instagram, the initial objective is to get followers so they can build a community of raving fans who will want to purchase their products and services. In order to build your community you must first learn how to increase your brand's exposure by getting more people to visit your Instagram page. The more people who visit your page the more followers you will obtain therefore increasing the influence of yourself and your brand which will allow you to create an asset that you can leverage to deliver value, market your products or services and ultimately grow your business and generate predictable profits. The most powerful marketing strategy you can utilize on Instagram to increase your page's exposure consists of leveraging the power of 'Instagram Influencers'. When done correctly, this can grow your Instagram following fast along with drive tons of warm leads to your website or sales funnel on a consistent basis.

The process by which you can leverage an Instagram Influencer's community to promote your page, product or service all begins with what is called a 'shoutout'. A shoutout involves sharing a post to feature another page or product ("go follow this person" or "go buy this product"). Since the beginning of Instagram, this is one of the most basic ways through which you can increase your following and sell your products and services on Instagram without needing to go through Facebook's confusing ad platform. You simply connect with an Instagram Influencer, pay them to post a screenshot of your page or share a post with your product in it along with a personal endorsement that encourages people to buy your product or service or follow your page.

The concept of 'influencer marketing' did not originate on Instagram, it is widely used through almost every type of media where marketers spend their time. Yet to this day using Instagram Influencers to build a community and drive traffic remains an overlooked and drastically misunderstood strategy by the vast majority of marketers. Their lack of awareness of the raw power of Instagram only makes it easier for people like you to take advantage of this great opportunity and begin using Instagram as an asset to launch and grow your business faster than ever before. Leveraging Instagram Influencers is very simple in nature but to understand the fundamentals along with the specific time-tested techniques we are going to need to dive deep into the overall strategy one step at a time. Whether you are looking to grow your follower base, drive traffic to your website or sales funnel or accomplish both of these objectives simultaneously, there are multiple free and paid strategies that you can begin utilizing today. So let's break them down beginning with the free strategies for growing your follower base.

SHOUTOUT-FOR-SHOUTOUT (S4S)

One of the most vast ways people build their communities on Instagram is by using a shoutout-for-shoutout or what some people refer to as a share-forshare (S4S). The way this works is you find a page with a similar follower base (in terms of niche and follower count) and you shoutout each other's Instagram page. You are essentially partnering with another Instagram page with the objective of tapping into their community to increase your brand's exposure and attract new followers. The process by which you introduce your brand to your shoutout partner's community is simple and incredibly easy to execute. You create a piece of branded and value based content that the person's audience/followers you are partnering with would benefit from. Beyond the highly visual image you want to create a compelling caption that entices their followers to visit your page and follow you. Make sure your Instagram username is in the first line of the caption to make it easy to view without having the user expand the caption in order to see your Instagram name.

When you are forming partnerships with people on Instagram for the purpose of doing a shoutout-for-shoutout the key component that drives this relationship is 'an equal exchange of value'. You want to be sure that when you are establishing a shoutout partnership both you and the person you are going to be shouting out are benefitting equally. If someone has half your follower base, they need to do 2 shoutouts for each one you post for them. So for example, if you have 3,000 followers and someone with 1,500 followers reaches out to you for a shoutout partnership, they would need to do 2 shoutouts in exchange for you giving them one shoutout.

When you have the right partnerships, shoutout-for-shoutouts can be an extremely effective way to increase the exposure of your page and increase your follower base quickly. That being said, there is a method to expand your reach without increasing your efforts. This can be done through shoutout groups.

SHOUTOUT GROUPS

Shoutouts groups, or what is also referred to as 'shoutout trains' leverage the power of a group of Instagram pages to multiply the exposure for everyone involved. Essentially, a group of active users will get together and start a 'train' where an individual gives a shoutout to one of the members in the group, followed by the second person shouting out the first person, followed by the third person shouting out the second person, and so on. All of this happens within a short period of time and it takes advantage of the snowball effect, where you are tapping into a ton of Instagram users.

You will notice that as you grow your following and work with Instagram users who have larger follower bases, the effect continues to compound. You tap into a larger base of Instagram users, which means more followers for your page. In turn, once your Instagram account begins to grow in size, you become a more attractive prospect and people will invite you to join their shoutout groups. It's a self-fulfilling cycle that benefits you as you continue to grow your Instagram following. Shoutout partnerships and shoutout groups can be a great way to grow your Instagram page, but they can also be harmful to your long-term growth if they are used carelessly or too frequently. Remember your followers chose to follow you for YOUR content, not other people's.

A WARNING ABOUT SHOUTOUT-FOR-SHOUTOUT

(S4S) You may be tempted to do a shoutout-for-shoutout with someone who has a larger follower base than you but has content that will not add value to your followers. If you choose to accept shoutout partners like this, you will hurt your brand and possibly lose the followers you worked hard to attract. On the other hand, the content you create for your shoutout partner's page should add value to their followers as well. Just remember, always deliver value and always keep your community in mind before you set up a new partnership.

Branding is E-V-E-R-Y-T-H-I-N-G on Instagram so proceed with caution before you partner with anyone on Instagram with the objective of trading shoutouts.

Although the above strategies are effective when used properly and cost little or nothing to utilize, they are not the fastest way to grow your follower base. The core strategy for growing your follower base extremely fast is simple – you pay Instagram Influencers to promote your Instagram page.

PURCHASING SHOUTOUTS FOR FOLLOWERS

Now this differs from the techniques previously mentioned because this will require an actual investment. You are essentially purchasing a shoutout from a page within your niche that is much larger than yours. Simply put, you are buying time on an Instagram Influencer's newsfeed and therefore increasing the exposure for your page. If you provide great content on your page more people will be compelled to follow you because they see value.

This strategy is one of the best if you are looking to grow your follower base quickly simply because you can focus on purchasing shoutouts from pages that are much larger than yours and you don't have to worry about an equal value exchange in terms of their follower base since you are paying for the shoutout. This will also protect your own brand since you have no obligation to share another Instagram users content.

Here are six ways people are using Instagram Influencers to grow their Instagram following:

1. The Instagram Influencer takes a screenshot of your page and features your last 9 images on their page and in the caption tells people to follow you.

2. The Instagram Influencer takes one of your original posts, copies it or redesigns it and features it on their page and tells their followers to follow you.

3. The Instagram Influencer creates their usual branded content but gives you a shoutout in the caption.

4. The Instagram Influencer posts your Instagram name on their story feature and tells people to follow you.

5. The Instagram Influencer does a live video telling people to follow you and pins your Instagram name on a comment while they are doing the live video.

6. The Instagram Influencer does a video telling people to follow you and posts it to their story.

When you use the paid shoutout strategy, make sure you choose an Instagram Influencer that has a substantial following. Anyone who has less than 100,000 followers is not going to send many people to your page. I suggest when you are getting started with paid shoutouts you look for Instagram pages that have 100k to 200K followers so you can test the engagement and the amount of followers you get. You can expect to incur anywhere from $20 (100k to 300K) to $300 (1M and up) for a paid shoutout and obviously the bigger the page the more followers you will attract. Understand that your shoutout only needs to be up for a few hours to be effective. So when you're negotiating prices a great strategy to use when the Instagram Influencer comes back with their fee is to request only a 6 hour shoutout to cut the cost down some.

PURCHASING SHOUTOUTS FOR TRAFFIC

Although growing your follower base is vitally important to your long-term success on Instagram, there is a way you can achieve consistent growth while driving traffic to your website or sales funnel at the same time. This topic is by far where I see most people go wrong and it's also the topic that I get the most questions about. So you are going to love to read this part slowly and carefully. Similar to shoutouts that help you grow your page, you simply find an Influencer on Instagram in your niche that has a massive community and get them to promote your service or product directly. You aren't focused on followers though – you aren't promoting your brand, rather, you are using them as promotional partners so that you can get your product/service/business in front of the right people for more sales, clients, leads, emails and profits.

After years of hard work, and consistently providing free value, many Instagram Influencers have built massive communities. The Influencers have trust, loyalty and credibility built with their followers. Many of the people who follow these large pages look to the Instagram page owner with celebrity status. They have thousands and thousands of people who are not only interested in following their page for the value the Instagram Influencer provides but are also willing to take it a step further. The Influencer's followers are actively looking for solutions to their problems and if you choose the right pages to promote with you can easily market your products or services (solutions) directly to their community. If you structure your promotions effectively, you can collect emails, generate leads, sell your products and generate consistent profits.

The huge advantage you have when choosing to market your products or services directly through Influencer promotions is two fold:

1. You create an instant spike of traffic to your website or sales funnel which will result in the collection of emails, leads and/or sales. At the very least, you will be able to test your website or sales funnel in only a few hours and use the data to improve your overall conversion rates.

2. You are still promoting your Instagram brand therefore you will grow your follower base at the same rate, if not faster than if you chose to promote just your page instead of a product or service.

Simply put, if you choose to promote your page with an Influencer and you purchase a shoutout you will gain followers. But if you choose to promote a product or service you will gain the same, if not more followers and you will be growing your email list, generating leads and making sales. The direct monetization aspect of promoting your products or services with Influencers should not be ignored which is why I consider this strategy to be the most powerful way of building your business on Instagram.

When you are selecting an Influencer to promote your products or services, make sure you choose one who has a large following. Getting someone who only has 50,000 followers will not be very effective. You should be looking for Instagram accounts who have at least 100,000 followers or more, anything less will not drive much traffic to your website or sales funnel nor will it get you many followers. On occasions, you can use smaller pages for quickly testing your promotions/shoutouts. This gives you the chance to make adjustments to your website or sales funnel before you commit large sums of money to your promotions. This is a great way to start out with your first few shoutouts and it can perhaps turn into a partnership once the Instagram account grows in size.

You can also consider to pay a little more for the Instagram Influencers who put the link to your website or sales funnel directly in their bio. Although this adds an extra cost to the promotion, I have found this to be the best strategy because it increases the amount of traffic to your website or sales funnel dramatically (as much as 314%). Once you have a selling process that is converting the Instagram followers of pages who have 100,000 to 300,000 followers into buyers, reach out to Instagram pages that have around 500,000 to 800,000 followers. Pages this size on Instagram should send about 500 to 700 visitors to your website or sales funnel and get you about 200 to 300 followers on your own

Instagram account. When you purchase promotions from Instagram accounts this size you can expect to pay about $60 for a shoutout that does not have your link in the Instagram Influencers bio and about $85 when your link is placed in the Influencers bio.

Instagram Influencers who have a million followers or more can be expensive to buy shoutouts from. However, these large Instagram pages will give you the best return on your investment when your website or sales funnel is fully optimized and converting visitors into customers. You will get the most amount of traffic and you will make back many times more than what you paid for the promotion/shoutout. These larger pages have higher credibility and many of the smaller pages' followers will follow the large Instagram pages as well so you'll have a better chance of doubling, tripling or even quadrupling your investment when you promote with these large Instagram pages (as long as your sales funnel is converting.

When you are testing shoutouts and promotions for the first time, you want to post on several different Instagram Influencer pages. All you do here is provide the Influencers you are promoting with the SAME message and the SAME photo. Make certain you do not run a shoutout at the same time on multiple pages and if you do, be sure to use tracking software that will allow you to gage how each shoutout performed. That way you know who to buy more from and who to buy less from or which pages to avoid working with altogether.

CONNECTING WITH INSTAGRAM INFLUENCERS

Your ability to set up profitable promotions that drive traffic to your page and your website or sales funnel will depend on your ability to connect with and partner with the right Instagram Influencers. You must first determine if they are willing to promote your page, product or service. The majority of time, when these Influencers are promoting something you'll see it right away when you read their bio. You can also see if they are sharing other brand's content on their page which is a good indication that they might be open to a shoutout partnership or be willing to sell you shoutouts for your page, product or service.

INSTAGRAM MARKET RESEARCH

Before you can even assess an Instagram Influencer's page to discover if they might be open to promoting your brand, product or service you must identify which communities on Instagram will resonate with you and your brand. This is vitally important to your overall strategy, especially if you are promoting your product or service directly since you must take more critical steps in order to maximize your traffic. Which market is your brand, product or service best suited for? Use the search function to input search terms that are relevant to your business and your niche. You will inevitably find big communities within your market. However, you don't want to get too focused with this because 'niches' on Instagram can be far more broad than you might expect. For example, motivational pages can attract network marketers, entrepreneurs, business owners and many diverse groups of people. When in doubt, put yourself in your customer's shoes and try to see what pages they would follow. You might have to do some research if you are having trouble with this step but believe me, it will be well worth it. Focus on collecting a wide range of smaller pages and larger pages. The smaller pages will be ideal for shoutout-for-shoutout partnerships since they will probably be around the same size as your page. They can even be used as test runs for when you start promoting your product or service since you will pay a much lower price when compared to the bigger pages.

Once you have finished your market research and have a few pages you would like to promote with you will want to reach out to these large Instagram pages. They will typically have some contact information in their bio – email or KIK (Warning: Their Instagram username might be different from their KIK name). Sometimes you can direct message (DM) them although most Instagram Influencers don't read their direct messages. If you are interested in finding shoutout-for-shoutout partners you can simply send them a personal message and see if they will be interested in working with you. If you are looking to expand your partnerships by using shoutout groups the same logic applies – send a personal message to 15 active Instagram accounts. You want anywhere between 10 to 15 people per shoutout group.

When you're reaching out to Instagram Influencers to purchase shoutouts always begin the conversation with a sincere compliment about their page and the content they provide. Ask them for their pricing and their packages (if they have any). Something simple like "Hey, I love your IG page and was wondering if you offered paid shoutouts and if so, what are your rates?" will suffice. Or, you can ask them if they are open for a shoutout-for-shoutout (S4S) if your following is similar to theirs. Always remember: Short, sweet and simple is best. Be yourself and see if you can negotiate the price down. Remember, they are selling air. Let the Instagram Influencer know if the shoutout you purchase from them is successful you would be willing to purchase 5 or 10 more if they could work with you on the price a bit. However, try not to haggle too much on this. They are spending their time and effort to help you out. Also, never assume they will give you a shoutout free of charge. Your default assumption should be that you are going to have to pay for it.

HOW TO BUILD YOUR BRAND

INDIVIDUAL BRANDING - THE POWER OF YOU

Because you have a LinkedIn profile doesn't mean your own marking endeavors are finished, be that as it may, you're set for an extraordinary beginning! An incredible beginning in view of LinkedIn's participation base (around 200 million), convenience and perhaps the most significant explanation: the inserted quest highlights which take into consideration a heap of ways for YOU to be found (or found). Having a finished profile and expert headshot on LinkedIn is a mammoth advance toward conveying your image. In any case, since you manufactured it doesn't mean they will come... so what's straightaway?

In case you're similar to numerous individuals, you're additionally on Facebook, Twitter, Google+, Pinterest, Instagram and a bunch of other systems administration related locales. You may not be as dynamic as some you know, however chances would you've say you've are in any event set up a profile to perceive what they're about right? Perhaps you've even made a Klout record to quantify your "social impact" on a scale from 1-100.

Have you transferred your photograph to Gravatar and enlisted on Google Profiles to make yourself progressively "discoverable" in the web indexes like Google, Bing and Yahoo? Have you wandered over to GoDaddy and bought your name as a website (or .net, .me, or the majority of the accessible augmentations)? Talking about URL possession, in the event that you haven't done so as of now, verify you alter and guarantee your name on your LinkedIn URL while it's still accessible. Snap on "Alter Profile" on your LinkedIn toolbar and just beneath your image you will see your LinkedIn address. Snap "alter" beside your location and look to the correct side of the page and snap on "Custom URL" and type in your favored name (without spaces). On the off chance that its accessible your location will presently be linkedin.com/in/yourname rather than the long series of numbers you were allotted of course. This will make you simpler to look in LinkedIn and encourage better web crawler results as you arrange your general marking endeavors.

In case you're similar to numerous individuals, you have a tad of yourself spread around in a few better places on the web making a much divided computerized impression. Chances are, every one of your own profiles are not as complete as they ought to be, your data is conflicting and this absence of composed exertion is smothering your own image adequacy and likely making for something not exactly ideal as far as outcomes when somebody types your name into one of the many web search tools. Also, a larger number of individuals than you may might suspect are looking through your name: companions, colleagues, new associates, business partners (previously, during or after the gathering), merchants, guardians in your no problem gathering, a forthcoming or current manager, an advisory group part, an enrollment specialist, etc, etc. you get the point, isn't that so? What's more, given the advancing proficiency of the web indexes and especially innovation like Facebook's new Graph Search, individuals can discover damn close to anything about you-the greater part of which you control however some you don't except if you find a way to quit open data aggregators like Spokeo. The main thing the matter is, YOU need to take control in the event that you need to impart a compelling individual brand.

Things being what they are, with a consistently expanding computerized impression, how would you organize your general nearness, move yourself up in the internet searcher standings and boost your own marking endeavors? The most proficient approach to achieve this is by utilizing one of a few individual marking destinations such as BrandYourself, Qnary (articulated like Canary) or About, just to name what I consider to be the best three decisions to help arrange and enhance your own image. These locales enable you to make an extensive profile by either moving data straightforwardly from LinkedIn on account of BrandYourself or simply reordering from your effectively finished LinkedIn profile for the others. When finished, everything has the presence of a customized site about you. In the event that you happen to claim your name as a website, you can go to "Area Management" on the GoDaddy webpage and forward yourname.com legitimately to your webpage of-decision address (ex: brand yourself.com/yourname) or for a little yearly expense Brand Yourself will veil your own URL and your Brand Yourself address will be yourname.com rather than brand yourself.com/yourname. It might sound more confounded than it is-it's in reality basic. With yourname.com as your customized site, you would now be able to include your URL your LinkedIn page under "Contact Info", your Facebook page under the "About" tab, Twitter, and pretty much whatever other webpage where the profile page takes into account an individual site.

Here's the truly cool part-the genuine reason for these individual marking locales is to interface the majority of your online exercises together under a center point and talked sort of methodology so as to augment your perceivability with the different web indexes. It functions admirably... I've done it thus can you! Every one of these destinations enable you to interface

Facebook, Twitter, LinkedIn, Gravatar, WordPress, Klout, Instagram, official statements, and pretty much whatever else you can consider to organize your online nearness and most significant, upgrading YOU with the different web crawlers. Keep in mind, be steady when finishing profile data about yourself. Be steady in verifying you investigate every possibility identified with your own marking endeavors and last, be quiet as it takes half a month to get brings about the different web crawlers. Your transient goal ought to be to show up on the primary page when your name is gone into any of the web indexes. The eventually goal obviously is to end up in the main position on the principal page of results! Hold tight... it very well may be finished!

Ways to Monitor and Protect Your Personal Brand

For the procedure of Personal Branding to be best, you have to give extraordinary consideration to observing and securing your image. It's a lot of like structure a house to live in-it's an awesome thing to bring the venture of developing the house as far as possible. Notwithstanding, when you need to utilize the house and need the experience to be to a lesser extent an issue and a greater amount of solace and satisfaction, you have to do periodical evaluation and review so you can manage any issues that may manifest and can be the premise of a bigger cerebral pain. The equivalent is valid for your Personal Brand. You have to screen and ensure your Personal Brand in the event that you need it to work for you most adequately over the long haul.

Here are some helpful hints you should consider:

Online Care

1. Google yourself routinely.

Some do it consistently, some week by week, month to month or even like clockwork. Contingent upon your field of work, your group of spectator's persona, and the online segment of what you do, it can vary enormously, yet it's constantly an unquestionable requirement. You ought to always remember to watch out for your most valuable vocation resource: your Personal Brand.

In the event that you have a typical name (John Smith) and there are bunches of other individuals with a similar name appearing in the consequences of your Google search, consider including your center name or utilizing an epithet or some other trick you may consider to isolate yourself from the carbon copies. It will clearly require some investment however it merits the exertion over the long haul.

Whenever you happen to discover data that isn't ideal about you, you have certain alternatives to consider:

Use SEO to further your potential benefit. The more applicable information you make containing your name, the more positive the Google results will be, on the grounds that Google adores new information and, therefore, your infamous information will be pushed down the query items further and further. Thus, invest some exertion and· dispatch your site utilizing a space under your own name (on the off chance that you don't as of now have one) compose sites with high thickness and recurrence of your preferred watchwords AND your name make new substance on your site normally by utilizing advertisements and furthermore fabricating association with different bloggers, increment the traffic to your site transfer proper photographs on the web with meta labels including your name

In the event that you'd like to know more, Brian Dean from Backlinko.com has great tips on this issue.

In the event that the issue is a result of some violation of social norms you have submitted, remain consistent with your real self and never attempt to conceal. Individuals may pardon you once, yet not over and again. Do a mea culpa, keep your fingers traversed with.

Set restricted access to your online networking profiles whenever the situation allows. Most interpersonal interaction destinations, for example, FB, LinkedIn and G+ let you do that.

Make a pledge so that starting now and into the foreseeable future you will be conscientious about what to digitize and what not to digitize. Security is brilliant nowadays, and once you've made the faux pas, the water is presumably under the extension. So reconsider before you post any content or picture on the web, anyplace.

Allow time to pass. Time is the healer everything being equal.In some cases, especially in outrageous cases, changing area or even your space may help.

Update your site and online life routinely.

Post drawing in material on your internet based life pages much of the time that will really increase the value of your group of spectators. Additionally, compose standard blog entries containing valuable substance that your group of spectators will need to peruse and share.

There is no ideal recurrence or number of posts that is substantial for everybody and there are huge amounts of variables that may impact the result. I propose you test, test and test. For instance, I've calculated the best recurrence of posting on Instagram for me is 1-2 posts for each day, and that I show signs of improvement results in the event that I post toward the evening time.

B: Offline Care

4. Concentrate on quality.

After some time, it's been demonstrated to me that competency is THE most significant factor in vocation achievement, considerably more than showcasing, attempts to sell something, and associations. To guarantee the best quality:

Continuously (finished) convey what you guarantee. Go the additional mile for your crowd.

Constantly plan your moves, measure your advancement, and right any issues.

Tune in to your group of spectators and act in like manner. All things considered, they are the individuals who put nourishment on your table.

Try not to sell yourself modest just in the quest for being increasingly unmistakable.

Concentrate resolutely on each objective in turn. Partitioning your consideration in such huge numbers of headings will just purpose disappointment.

5. Update yourself.

Every night, ask yourself "What have I adapted today?"

I generally start and finish my days with 30 min of perusing. Never stop to learn and apply your new information to your activity.

Be innovative to remain in front of copycats.

Go to workshops and join specific vested parties and relationship in your field.

6. Assess your Personal Brand.

Transient outcomes: Have I seen any outcomes during the previous 1-6 months?

Brand mindfulness: Are individuals increasingly mindful of who I am and what I do than previously?

Arriving at objectives: How much have I gone along the way of accomplishing my objectives?

C: One Other Important Tip

7. Manage individuals judiciously.

Adhere to the brilliant standard. Treat others as you might want to be dealt with.

Continuously regard your followers and fans and the individuals who remained alongside you at troublesome occasions.

Regard everybody in your system. I think a significant motivation behind why the vast majority of my rivals talk well despite my good faith is on the grounds that I generally demonstrate the most extreme regard for them, regardless of how experienced they are.

Disregard desirous individuals. Their envy is a striking marker that they trust you are superior to them.

Try not to think about negative remarks literally. Haters for the most part loathe themselves for not accomplishing the incredible things that you did. The most noticeably bad thing you can do with a contrary individual online is to attempt and 'right' their emotions about you and your substance. They have commonly decided on you and what you're doing as such there is almost no opportunity of persuading them generally. Rather, when you react to their criticism you're touching off their fire and demonstrating that you'll draw in with them. This opens the entryway for them to keep on having a great time at your record. They are out to provoke your feelings and when you react, particularly when you react with high feeling, you're giving them precisely what they need.

Keep in mind you are a good example. It doesn't make a difference if just a hundred people know you or you have a huge number of fans all through the world. In case you're trying to improve your own image, attempt to go about as though everybody's watching all of you the time. Serve individuals, provide for philanthropies, be unassuming, and your character will radiate through the group.

Why Instagram is so amazing for your business and individual brand

A considerable number of individuals now have found out about the little application called Instagram; that has overpowered the world. So it doesn't make a difference in the event that you are an innovation master, which thinks about the best in phone applications, or you can scarcely browse your email. So we would all be able to concur that somebody we know is consistently on Instagram. When you check out these days it's an uncommon sight if you don't see somebody glued to their telephone, totally not informed of what's happening around them. It's truly intriguing how much individuals make use of their telephone while in a discussion, now and then more centered on the telephone rather than the discussion they are having with the individual directly before them. So, has this at any point transpired, or possibly you even done this without anyone's help?

So, it's an alternate world we are living in now; instead of 10 - 20 years back. In those days cell phones weren't that smart, applications we not as pervasive, and people who where not completely entranced by their telephones, and all the more significantly, the applications they use on them. And nowadays you can use applications like Instagram to converse with sidekicks whether by naming them in something you saw, sending them a video message, offering an explanation to a story they posted, or even reliant on watching something that helped you to recall them. And you can likewise get made up for lost time investigating various urban areas, viewing your preferred on-screen character each day life, or your preferred humorist doing a live steam or some game features from a nights ago game. Be aware that none of this existed 15 years prior, in those days individuals would go to possibly the TV for excitement yet now individuals are expending more energy one their smartphones than any time in recent memory and Instagram is the place they are investing the greater part of their time. And regardless of whether you possess a business or need to assemble your own image. Therefore, Instagram is unquestionably one of the stages you have to use, here is the reason you can attach to that claim.

Do you know on Instagram you gain admittance to more than 800 million clients consistently? And Instagram is quickly ascending to the highest point of every single social medium stages, and with an astounding 800 million clients it has turned out to be probably the best stage with which to contact your focused crowd. You can meet your clients and individuals wherever they are. Meanwhile, at the present time, they are on Instagram, and their telephone making it significantly progressively incredible. By research, you can, for the most part, find someone looking at their phone, and even more fundamentally using Instagram.

Instagram makes Networking easier and straightforward for you. The systems administration abilities and broad arrive at that Instagram has given us, on a worldwide scale is unrivaled. Smart people realize they should make the most of each chance to develop and extend their system. And Instagram enables you to interface with individuals dependent on their inclinations, area, hash labels and shared companions and contacts. And the best thing is that you can reach the globe from your cell phone. And presently this really gives you a valid justification for all the time you spend on Instagram.

Instagram expands your compass and commitment. Instagram has multiple times more reach and devotee commitment than Facebook, and a shocking multiple times more reach than Twitter. So assembling your Instagram group of spectators is crucial to your prosperity now and significantly more so in the coming future. If that you're not building your focused on crowd (individuals who are keen on your individual brand or business) it's practically similar to not having a PDA or email for individuals to get in touch with you. And this can be likened to a fisher men not having an angling rod post or net to catch fish, a hairdresser not having scissors to trim hair, we're certain you get the point at this point. Start assembling your group of spectators today so you can begin picking up force and introduction quick setting you up for the future with a strong foundation to expand upon.

Instagram is simple to utilize and generally for fun. For individuals who know about Instagram, you definitely realize how fun and simple it is to utilize. And regardless of whether you at present have an individual or a business record you presumably as of now see how ground-breaking Instagram can be. Individuals can investigate various urban communities, nations, and landmasses directly from their telephone and furthermore observe and do live recordings for their group of spectators. You can as well go along with somebody on a live video, talk with style. What's more, the conceivable outcomes are huge with new component being included frequently. Instagram also enables you to essentially have a TV coordinate without the TV system cost. Surprisingly better you can get live and instant criticism from your crowd with remarks and commitment directly as you are conversing with them that is more dominant than TV.

For the individuals who in one way or the other haven't used Instagram, it very well may be an astounding thing to do. It allows you to associate with individuals or a group of spectators that is exceptionally engaged. You can construct a group of people that is nearby, across the country, or global relying upon your inclination; image, callings, or energy. And there is a familiar axiom, " words usually can't do a picture justice." So start make use of Instagram today, and let your photos state a large number of words for you. People have continually loved pictures for a very long time so you know Instagram will be here for the entire arrangement.

Utilizing Instagram you can make significant associations.

A considerable number individuals know now Instagram has been growing altogether. Everybody realizes somebody that is consistently busy with their telephone checking their Instagram, and all the more critically Instagram holds individuals' consideration. And it has become a stage that individuals and organizations can use to interface with others. So would you be able to envision interfacing with new individuals and potential clients ordinary just from utilizing Instagram? Consider the possibility that you had the choice to build up a rich, significant, association with your group of spectators. Simultaneously make and build up your very own image and nearness in the psyches of individuals everywhere throughout the world. Also additionally to keep awake to date with loved ones, Instagram really enables you to do everything and that's only the tip of the iceberg.

It is imperative to develop your group of spectators on Instagram, however becoming your Instagram yourself is hard with the consistently evolving calculation. It makes it significantly harder for you to develop your calendar. So you can post content day by day and you probably won't see the kind of development you anticipated. [http://www.Myinstagrow.com] was made to supercharge your Instagram, and free up your valuable time to concentrate on your enthusiasm, your business, image, and what you specialize in. The vast majority see somewhere in the range of 200-2000 new focused on adherents every week relying upon your post content, administration bundle, and set up. The individuals pulled in to your Instagram will be individuals that are keen on you, what you do, and your energy.

Tips on Using Instagram for Your Brand-Building

Step by step instructions to Create a Powerful Instagram Social Media Marketing Strategy

One of the most dominant promoting apparatuses advertisers have today is online life. From Facebook presents on tweets on Twitter, sharing your items or administrations via web-based networking media stages is an extraordinary method to build brand mindfulness, commitment, deals and leads.

Meanwhile, numerous individuals are left scratching their heads with regards to showcasing with Instagram.

A considerable lot of us use Instagram as an individual record to post photographs of our family, companions, getaways and nourishment - yet how might it tie into business? What's more, would it be advisable for it to?

So with the speed at which Instagram is developing, don't disparage its incentive to help your image and showcasing endeavors.

It has developed into an amazingly important advertising stage and despite the fact that the 18-multiyear olds are as yet pervasive clients, the higher age gatherings are getting on and making up for lost time quick.

What to mark in years to come – Instagram Hashtags

• 8 out of many hashtags like 10 are marked on Instagram

• 80% of clients pursue a business on Instagram

- 65% of top-performing Instagram posts include items

So in the event that you feel the pull to investigate Instagram as a component of your web based life promoting methodology, look at these underlying pointers to enable you to begin:

1. Use Hashtags Wisely

You don't have to jampack each hashtag you can consider in one post, however you do require in any event a couple.

A hashtag is the # sign pursued by unmistakable words about your picture as in this model, I utilized #marketing and #ctaconf, which was the gathering I was going to at the time.

And at the point when a client clicks/taps on a hashtag or types a hashtag into the inquiry put away, it raises all pictures that made use of that hashtag. The client can even buy in to keep on following that hashtag.

The expectation is the client will see your photograph, head to your profile and most ideal situation, tail you and get connected with a greater amount of your posts!

When hashtags are incredibly famous, the challenge to appear in the result is wild. Like SEO keywords, the more well known a term is, the difficult it is to remain at the highest point of the list items. In this manner, my case of utilizing #marketing truly was useless i I needed to get any footing from that post.

You need to make your hashtags applicable to your business and niche, yet in addition connecting enough that a client would type them into Instagram's hunt box.

For example:

• Or you're a Toronto wedding organizer. You post a picture of a lady of the hour and husband to be's first hit the dance floor with the hashtags #LoveWins #TorontoWeddingPlanner #WinterWedding

Occasions and exceptional occasions are a magnificent time to advance your business and increase Instagram adherents. Regardless of whether it's a deal on Black Friday, a Thanksgiving-related use for your item or an item yell out on National Dog Day, they are for the most part perfect chances to feature your business image in an appropriate way.

2. Say thanks to Your Audience for Showing Up

You don't simply post a lot of photographs and hashtags and trust that the preferences will come in.

To pick up Instagram followers, draw in with your group of spectators and develop deals or leads, you have to place in the time.

So, provided that somebody leaves a remark or question on one of your posts, set aside the effort to answer and express gratitude toward them/reply their inquiry.

Investigate their profile, and in the event that you love what you see, tail them.

Organizations frequently make use of analysts first, in the expectations that they may give back.

You can likewise look for individuals who may be keen on your item, at that point remark on their photographs as well as tail them, yet don't spam them with a request to tail you immediately.

3. Communicate with the Right Influencers

Influencers are Instagram users who can impact your intended audience or interest group as a result of their notoriety and additionally internet based life following.

That might be an extraordinary model, and except if you have profound pockets you likely won't have the option to draw in an influencer with right around 2,000,000 followers.

Be that as it may, don't surrender. From mother bloggers to nearby foodies, you can generally discover somebody who your intended interest group pursues, enjoys or respects. Possibly they'd be happy to survey your item or snap a picture utilizing it - utilize your creative mind!

4. Don't Just Shill Your Products

Instagram isn't the spot to just share item shots without planning. Think about the experience individuals have utilizing what you're offering, or the advantages it gives individuals.

Far and away superior, show genuine models. Requesting client created content from your crowd is one approach to do this. That implies that clients share their photographs by making use of a hashtag you give.

Make certain to tell individuals that their pictures may be included on your page and you can build your Instagram content no doubt - for nothing!

Regardless of how you use Instagram for your business, be genuine and consistent with your image. It's what the stage is about, and it will enable you to develop your business, gain Instagram followers and pull in deals or leads.

Instructions to Boost and Market Your Business: Instagram

Organizations making us of Instagram to advance their items, administrations and offers presently have a considerably more prominent chance to showcase their products to a super focused on crowd. Be aware that Instagram has recently propelled its promoting stage that coordinates with Facebook's astonishing focusing on capacities and organizations are exploiting with the sponsorship of Facebook. Therefore, Instagrammers are 2.5 occasions bound to tap on newsfeed advertisements than promotions on some other internet based life stage. Meanwhile, be aware that running Instagram advancements for your business open up a vast expanse of possibility.

Portable publicizing has outperformed paper promoting without precedent for history and huge and private ventures the same are accomplishing quantifiable outcomes with web-based social networking publicizing. Be aware that Instagram marketing has just produced the greater part a billion in income and is anticipated to multiply two times inside a year, which is evidence that numerous entrepreneurs are putting their cash where their mouth is.

All the more significantly Instagram promotion stage is anything but difficult to utilize, it's fun and rising over with energetic and eager clients. It has great measurements is as yet reasonable for private ventures. And when you are as of now promoting your item with internet based life advertisements or attempting to assemble your rundown at that point incorporating Instagram promotions into your showcasing blend is fundamental.

Below are five hints to consider before running a promotion on Instagram to develop your business image reach, connect with your followers, or draw in your intended interest group to your offer.

1. Get the rudiments right. Make it a point to utilize an unmistakable, fresh form of your organization logo as your profile picture.

2. Create a detailed description why you are on Instagram to your followers. And since this is a business account to work with, keep it business, not close to home. Always help clients relate to your image and simply try not to be too expensive.

3. Start with an arrangement. Strategize your Instagram (and all your online life) advancements by arranging them out. Making out for a schedule which further executes your objective is a brilliant way to have prospect for the business. Not having an arrangement is the primary motivation behind why organizations fail via internet-based networking media, so do this before you start posting arbitrarily or paying for traffic!

4. So always try not to let your hashtags be your voice. Rather, loan your business voice to your hashtags. Redo hashtags for marking purposes and for regular posting, keep them significant and within reach. It's extraordinary to utilize hashtags, simply make a point to not lose control and produce such a large number of in one post - convey quality over amount.

5. Update your look. Clever Instagram clients need to see "lovely" or read "amusing" or identify with something significant. Use applications and other picture or video apparatuses to overhaul the look and feel of all that you post on Instagram looking beautiful and professional for your brand ethics and recognition.

How Influencers Can Get Cut-Through On Instagram

Keep in mind the telephone directory? And it wasn't such a long time ago that when we required an assistance or item, we'd get the telephone directory and quest for a business that could support us.

Back then, the organizations that had success were the ones that had a name starting with "A". That is on the grounds that they would be at the highest point of the A-Z postings. Individuals would be bound to call A-Plus Plumbers instead of W&W Plumbing Services, for instance.

In any case, that is altogether changed. Telephone directories are a relic of days gone by. Disregard A-Z postings - the organizations that succeed today are the ones that top internet based life sustains.

To be discovered, you should be via internet-based networking media. Also, one of the most dominant online networking stages is Instagram. It's the main web based life platforms that nearly ensures your profile a spot at the highest point of the feed. That is on the grounds that Instagram has presented a component called Stories.

Stories breathes life into your image. It enables you to share and examine different photographs and recordings; each one of the snapshots of your day that consolidate to make up your one of a kind "story".

Recordings are significant with regards to building your own image. Unconstrained recordings are a viable type of documentation. They catch your musings as they occur and help you group your one of a kind substance - imperative for any Influencer.

In this way, it's nothing unexpected that Stories is demonstrating to be a pivotal brand-building device for Influencers. Late information demonstrates that while Facebook has the most active number of individuals in Australia, Instagram is the quickest developing interpersonal organization. Since stories was propelled in 2016, there's additionally been a decrease in Snapchat use - beforehand the main web-based social networking stage that enabled clients to post recordings "on the run".

Additionally, Instagram is driven by hashtags. This implies it acts like an internet searcher, so you're bound to turn up in list items when somebody is looking on the web for an efficient yours. It additionally utilizes area information, which is extraordinary news in case you're focusing on a group of people in a particular zone - for instance, in the event that you are a fitness coach in Brisbane.

Two different ways you can utilize Instagram furthering your potential benefit:

1. As a cleaned marking apparatus.
Stylised pictures and recordings can give your image a refined edge.

2. As an unconstrained catch device.

Recordings allow you to share the snapshots of your day as they occur. They give your group of spectators a one of a kind understanding into what your identity is, your specialty and how you can support them. It likewise demonstrates to them that no doubt about it individual, not just a message.

Exchange master Tony Perzow is an incredible case of somebody who uses Instagram recordings in a groundbreaking way. His recordings not just market his projects, they illuminate, engage and teach his group of spectators. Wholehearted Studio's Hayley Jenkin is another business person who uses Instagram uncommonly well. Her pictures and recordings are increasingly stylised and intentionally made, ideal for structure her photography business' modern image.

Be attentive, in any case, of making progress toward flawlessness. Business people frequently have a dread of seeming inauthentic or "flashy". Web based life can be a genuine battle for them, so they avoid any risk and sit idle. Thus, their rivals show up at the highest point of their spectators' online life bolsters. They're the ones who have an effect and get the leads.

Be daring. To be an Influencer, you should grasp web based life. Try not to get hung up about seeming impeccable - individuals need to see the genuine you. Recordings can give you tremendous slice through with your crowd. Even better, you don't have to spend colossal measures of cash or have an expert chronicle studio. In such manner, Instagram presents the ideal partner.

Using Instagram: Tips For Promoting Your Brand

Be aware that Instagram is one of the most dominant versatile applications that enable you to share photographs, recordings or accomplish a lot more things either openly or secretly. It was founded in the year 2010 by Kevin Systrom and Mike Krieger. In view of its notoriety, its number of clients quickly increments once a day. These days, it is broadly used to develop a business or to drive deals. It expands your adherents who are really keen on your items and administrations. When you are new to Instagram, don't have to stress yourself. And this is on the grounds that here in this book, we secured all focuses, which you should know to promote your image worldwide and to build your deal. How about we begin.

Make your different character: If you need to advance your image on Instagram, along these lines, as a matter of first priority, you need to make your different personality on it. And for this, you simply need to make another business account, which is thoroughly isolated from your own record.

Incorporate a connect to raise traffic: Another most straightforward approach to advance your image over the Instagram is by adding your site connect to it. It allows you to legitimately lead a potential client over to your site. This will assist your devotee with landing your site legitimately without confronting any issue.

Incorporate a useful bio to snare your devotees: You ought to consistently remember that your adherent will initially experience your profile, if that they appear it intriguing or useful, at that point just they will begin tailing you. So this will assist you with promoting your items and administrations or your image name also.

Upgrade your pictures to stick out: Instagram consequently makes your photograph square; you simply need to edit it expertly, so it can undoubtedly catch the eye of the supporter and they will begin getting connected with you. You ought to consistently utilize quality photographs of your offered items and administrations to drive deals or for its advancement also.

That is all, what you have to advance your image on Instagram. As a web based life administrator, you ought to comprehend the intensity of Instagram and use it as needs be to get more outcomes. This is probably the least demanding approaches to get connected with your devotees, you simply need to realize how to really utilize it. And every above point will help in this. Continuously recall showcasing isn't for you, it's for your crowd, along these lines, think from their viewpoint, in this way, that your endeavors will never get squandered.

The most effective method to Get Your Business Booming On Instagram

Instagram has more than 700 million clients on a month to month basis. Studies reveal that clients are multiple times bound to interface with a mark symbol on Instagram opposed to what Facebook entails, and multiple times bound to make some move than individuals on Twitter.

Your business can possibly arrive at a colossal number of people in various territories over the globe with Instagram.

Beginning With Instagram

In the first place, get the application from Stores like Google Play store or Apple store. And you'll have the decision to make an individual or business profile. Decide for the business profile. Instagram conveys some showcasing and conduct following apparatuses for business profile account holders.

Make Content

Instagram is a photograph sharing site. It's imperative to distribute remarkable, quality substance on the off chance that you need your business blast on Instagram. Instagram is about lovely and eye-getting pictures. Be aware that extraordinary photographs or recordings can help flash enthusiasm for your business and attract individuals. Up your game by adapting some photography aptitudes. So post limited time refreshes after about each 4 or 5 instructive updates.

Commitment

Always make use of hashtags to get to the individuals you eventually need to work with. Attempt to use terms and expressions in your substance that your intended interest group will look for. Put aside time to remark, as, and connect with your devotees all the time.

Loads of information shows that the best time to post on Instagram is at 5pm on Wednesdays. Be that as it may, this may or probably won't be right for your page dependent on your topic, the socioeconomics of your devotees and different things explicit to your market and substance material.

Investigation

Investigating your promoting on Instagram is extremely straightforward. This is all the significant information about your page.

So look at what number of new adherents you get and how a lot of commitment you get. And before excessively long, you'll see what sorts of pictures get the most likes and the most remarks. Start taking a greater amount of those kinds of photographs, or assembling them on the web.

Setting a pace for your brand on Instagram

As a rousing business person you have heard it from numerous sources: you have to jump via web-based networking media and make a substantial nearness. Well that is more difficult than one might expect. You pick Instagram in light of the fact that it's straightforward and may you have an individual record. You know you're route around and sign up. Presently what? You see garish vehicles, lovely scenery's, and uber effective individuals demonstrating their way of life off. Is that what I do, or is something more to this stage?

First how about we take a gander at what effective individuals do

When you take a gander at any effective individual you see quickly how they dress, hold themselves, walk, talk, and so forth... It is the sort of people they are and how they characterize themselves. More than likely they are uber sure, direction consideration when they talk, and are held in high respect. They don't must have the cleanest suit you at any point looked at, or that fantasy vehicle you generally wish you had, however inside a couple of moments you realize what they are about. They offer extraordinary worth, show themselves in an individual issue, help other people arrive at the top and so forth...

Presently we should see a few "characters"

All of you know them, they either post some insane get-away constantly, gaudy autos, cash, and so on yet, you realize regardless they live at home. You know what this does? It totally decimates one's close to home brand and notoriety. They are fundamentally telling individuals they are faking it until they make it.

Presently it's your turn

Once you know that you're simply considering going into business or individual Instagram account and have ONE chance to demonstrate the world a look into your existence, just do it. Try not to go super only for preferences, be authentic, powerless, and welcoming to other individuals. Offer extraordinary incentive by offering incredible guidance or tips. Help individuals when they didn't request it. Show individuals what you are as of now dealing with in your business. Try not to spam you item or be irritating to your adherents. Show individuals your distinction in your specialty to stand apart more and demonstrate your own image the genuine you. Structure an arrangement around what your general message will be to your adherents. Knowledge on your business, significant hints and deceives, colossal worth bombs, incline ups for item dispatches, and so on.

Instagram: The Rise and its impact on the profitability of your Business

The Rise of Instagram.

Why?

Since 2010, Instagram has demonstrated itself to be the quickest developing web-based social networking stage around! And it has a client base of around 300 million and that is set to rise further. And when everything comes down to innovativeness truly, Instagram have discovered better approaches for sharing substance over its foundation and making clients experience increasingly consistent.

Be aware that Instagram now has more influence over the entirety of its clients who may have been utilizing snapchat couple to its own application, diminishing the need to utilize both and stream coating these clients to its very own administrations.

Instagram stories likewise empower additionally sharing of substance and giving it a conversation component to its application, enabling it to contend with the various direct informing stages. Development like this is the explanation behind Instagram's abrupt development and innovation.

What's everything you still need to know?

Be aware that Instagram is the ideal application to share content through visual symbolism. Its crowd are youthful, instructed and excited about shopping. And this makes the content inventive, energizing and quick moving. And be aware that it has an alternate vibe to stages like Facebook and Twitter, with spotlight on visuals as opposed to words. Nonetheless, considers have demonstrated that, as Facebook, it is utilized day by day, this makes for a faithful and profoundly dynamic client base.

This capacity to catch a more youthful increasingly innovative group of spectators is sounding the alerts of significant organizations hoping to publicize via web-based networking media. With high utilization, there will without a doubt be expanded enthusiasm for promoting on the platform. Nonetheless, rivalry will be ready and organizations should discover inventive approaches to out perform their adversaries in the visual universe of web based life.

How might You use it for Marketing?

Obviously, if you wish to utilize this to promote your organization or an item, at that point one must think about how. This is a visual stage and consequently items are when all is said in done simpler to showcase that administrations. Be that as it may, administrations are not difficult to advance on the application, finding energizing approaches to enliven your administration will grab the attention of the Instagram client.

Hashtags are as often as possible utilized on Instagram and getting in on patterns or in any event, beginning your own is a certain method to connect with a group of people, along these lines to Twitter. Nonetheless, one must be mindful so as to plan the hashtag to the visual content you give, so it isn't as basic as different applications that utilization this system.

Instagram is predominately a portable application, so substance must be anything but difficult to use and persistently refreshed for a versatile information, hungry statistic. Just new and new substance will stand out.

At long last, Instagram stories are an extraordinary method to actually draw in with your group of spectators, enduring just 24 hours. Meanwhile, stories ought to be used in a way to keep potential clients refreshed every day on your business and uncover in the background substance to make the client feel like they are a piece of the organization.

Instagram can be utilized to advertise nearly anything, with an inventive personality and a submitted group, you can make an incredible buzz around your image!

The Future

With a youthful, instructed group of spectators utilizing the application on their mobiles day by day, one can just anticipate supported development and unwaveringness from its clients. There will expand chance to utilize this application for business purposes and the guidance from this author is to get in while its hot! It will just get greater so get into the commercial center before it gets considerably progressively swarmed.

HOW TO USE INSTAGRAM VIDEOS FOR BUSINESS

There exist no limitation to what you can do with Instagram video posts, all in a bid to let your Instagram followers catch real-time events of your day to day activities; which is why it is so easy to find them on your feeds.

That being said, for Instagram to work for you and your business, need to have clear objectives as to why you want to use the digital tools made available on the platform; whether it is to communicate your brand message for more awareness, promote your goods and services, or incorporate your Brand name to the Instagram community. You can visit the site to check videos of various brands to see how successful they have been and learn a thing or two from them. Below are a few things they use of Instagram videos can do for your brand.

Promoting your products

Because videos can convey a ton of information within a short time and they are attractive to viewers who are always eager to see the end of what your videos are about, they are an enormous asset for businesses selling products or services primarily when used for adverts.

Just imagine how many more of your goods you can view in a 60-second video compared to viewing only one image!

According to Hubspot, after watching a video of a product for the first time, 64% of customers are more likely to buy that product online. And seeing your goods on display using Instagram videos could be a significant way to increase your ROI based on Instagram advertising alone! Can you beat that?!

Building Brand Trust

Sharing videos on Instagram that projects your brand message and show your business culture is a great way to build trust with your teeming fans and customers. An excellent example from @foodora.ca shows how lovely their meal delivery system can be. This meal-delivery company also shares and gives value to engaging video content that is important to their target market.

Teach Your Audience

Do you have any topic which you would like to teach your target audience, that will excite them and generate their interests in learning? Maybe it is a tasty cake recipe or a makeup tutorial? Whatever your concentration, sharing short, educational content using Instagram video posts is a great strategy. The point here is, if you have a fascinating subject you feel you would enjoy learning about it, it is a great strategy to use Instagram videos to do it. You could conduct a poll with about three topics, so you get to know firsthand what the majority of your fans are interested in learning, not only because you love that particular topic.

Ready to start preparing Instagram videos?

Get on with it. Look for a beautiful scene, bright workspace and shoot a simple video and watch the reactions from your followers. Whatever it is, decide to do better with every video! That was easy, right?! Now that we have discussed how to share your Instagram videos let's take a minute to explore how you can refine your video content to get more traction.

Pick an Eye-Catching Cover Photo

In our world today, where attention span is becoming increasingly scarce, it can be quite challenging to gain your followers to interact with your videos (especially the very longer videos). So, having a great cover photo is one great way to get their attention and improve your chances of having them stick around on your page.

Just as you are spending time finding pictures that look good on your feed, you also need to spend a lot of time finding a high cover image for your video. Otherwise, all the hard work you put into creating your video will be a waste! Try to find a picture that reflects your video's overall message when choosing a cover photo and also, one that has the best image quality to stop viewers from scrolling past your content.

Don't Rely on Sound

Don't rely on Instagram sound videos in the feed to play automatically; viewers will have to click on the video to hear music. However, even when they don't play a sound, let the video itself speak volumes about what you are trying to sell or project. Since you are trying to capture people's attention in the first couple of seconds, it is essential to keep in mind that even without audio, your videos need to be clearly understood!

In all, your videos should be as stunning as the images used to see your followers on your page. Even if your audience doesn't have the overall effect, you want them to see the Instagram video plot— even if it is quiet.

Focus on the First Few Seconds Your Video

With so much to see on Instagram, producing video content that catches the attention of people within the first 3-5 seconds is vital. By concentrating on your video's first few seconds and making them great, you are sure to get high-quality leads and engagement.

Choose a video length that works for your audience

Just because the duration of your Instagram videos can be as long as 60 seconds doesn't mean it should be the norm for all your videos. Like all social media stuff, keeping the audience engaged over a more extended period is challenging.

To find the video duration that works best for your audience, consider experimenting with different video lengths. Focus on creating shorter video content if you find useful metrics on your clips that are below 30 seconds. If your clips are longer than your shorter ones, stick with them.

Use a third-party app to Revamp your Instagram video.

There are plenty of apps and tools you can utilize to not only improve the quality of your videos, but also add branding to them, whether it is your logo, font, or some other design feature.

Instagram Stories Business

This is where your creativity has to be topnotch! Instagram Stories have become a vital part of your Instagram marketing strategy since they first arrived on the scene in 2017. In reality, 64 percent of companies are planning to create more Instagram Stories in 2018, according to The State of Instagram Marketing 2018.

So what explains the enormous success of Instagram Stories? Okay, it partially has to do with ephemeral video's growing popularity. More and more companies see the importance of producing short-lived video content, whether it is entertaining, lighthearted, or business related.

Here's How To Use Instagram Stories For Business:

Unlike regular Instagram picture posts, Instagram would not penalize you for posting too many Instagram stories— and this is because Instagram stories are short with a transient nature. Since Instagram Stories live for 24 hours (or forever if you share them as highlights of Instagram Stories for as long as you like), there is not much pressure on the social channel to prioritize any posts on a user page over others. Of course, that doesn't mean that the Instagram algorithm doesn't influence Instagram stories because they're certainly doing, and we don't have control over the algorithm!

It is just that the number of stories you share doesn't seem to have a significant impact on how many people will view your Instagram stories. According to Hat, if you post tons and tons of stories every day, there's a very high probability that at least few of your followers will mute your account on their devices!

That doesn't mean it is a bad thing to post a lot of Instagram stories. It comes down to the quality and authenticity of materials you post regularly! Several accounts can get away with publishing 10 + stories a day, while others are better off posting just a few days a week. Although posting for some accounts works multiple times a day, it may not work for you. Creating more than 10 Instagram Stories can take a lot of time and planning, especially to get the kind of quality content you plan to deliver to your fans. So if you feel your time is best spent elsewhere, it is probably best to stick to a few stories a week, and your fans will be just fine!

Therefore, when you post a lot of stories regularly, your fans will expect you to continue to do so; if you leave them hanging, they will go elsewhere to fill the void. There is no "optimal" frequency for stories at the end of the day, but it is good to have enough to last for the week that people look forward to seeing your content without getting tired.

When Should You Post Instagram Stories?

It is imperative to post when your fans are most active when it comes to daily Instagram posts. But that's not the case for Instagram business and Instagram Stories. Since Instagram Stories live for up to 24 hours (again, that's if they're not posted as highlights), if you post a story, your followers have a 24-hour window at the top of their feeds.

So even if you post one Instagram story at a time when most of your followers are sleeping, when they wake up, they will still be able to find your story at the top of their feeds. In other words, you shouldn't stress too much about posting optimal times for your Instagram stories. In which case, posting while your followers are most engaged would help, unless you are looking for immediate interaction.

What to Post on Instagram Stories Like regular posts, it is good to post a mix of insightful, fun, and promotional content if you are using Instagram Stories for company. Instagram Stories is a relaxed place in particular, and the quality standards for regular posts are much lower than they are. So don't be scared or intimidated to show off your exciting attributes; you're only human!

The interesting thing about Instagram Stories is that you can become as imaginative as you like! And the same applies to Instagram Stories promotional material. Sharing promotional content, which is also fun and lighthearted, is simple.

In any case, keeping track of your Instagram Stories analytics is extremely important to see what kinds of content your audience can better react to. As we mentioned earlier, it signals to the algorithm that you are creating high-quality content when your stories accrues a lot of views and interaction, so that your potential Instagram stories can appear higher up in the queue of stories of your fans.

So you have a better opportunity of getting your future Instagram stories to be seen by more people by creating great Instagram stories material that your followers love!

Instagram Stories Features That Are Great For Business

When it comes to the use of Instagram Stories for business and Instagram ads, there are a few features that you can use to get the most quality target leads for the money you spend:

Location and Hashtag Stickers

When Instagram first launched Instagram Stories stickers in 2017, they were a lot more fun than being useful.

Since then, Instagram has introduced a ton of new functionality to stickers, including the ability to see location-based stories on the Explore page, and the ability to search for stories by location and hashtag was added quite recently.

To brands, these features have made an enormous difference in helping them achieve visibility on Instagram. While you were only able to share Instagram Stories with your followers at first, these new features allow anyone in the world to see your Instagram stories!

For example, if you post a story from an Atlanta restaurant, you can mark the location with a sticker, and your account may appear in the Instagram Stories at that location. The same applies to stickers with hashtags. It will appear on the corresponding hashtag site when a user marks a hashtag in their Instagram stories.

Clickable Links

Recently, Instagram Clickable Links rolled out the ability to add links to Instagram Stories, and it is quite a big deal! Yes, because this is the first time people have ever been able to add a reference to Instagram, which is not the connection in their profile! How cool is that?!

This goes without saying that it is highly beneficial to your business for Instagram ads to be able to send your followers prompts from your stories to different landing pages. You can use this function to push Instagram traffic to all sorts of related landing pages, whether it is a brand page or a new blog post!

Quick Tip: The call-to-action "See More" icon that appears on Instagram stories with clickable links is quite tiny and can quickly go unnoticed, so calling it out using text, arrows, or some other design feature is by far a good idea.

Tag Other Accounts

We are quite aware of how active Instagram contests are in driving engagements and getting new clients and followers, and with the option of tag other Instagram Stories accounts. There is another way to drive traffic to your posts; especially, If you are running a takeover or influencer campaign, tagging other accounts in your stories is also helpful.

Tag other Businesses in Your Sponsored Instagram Stories

The new paid collaboration feature of Instagram makes it super easy to tag brands in your sponsored Instagram Stories. So far, only a handful of celebrities, influencers, and businesses have been given access to the tool, but in the coming months, a larger-scale rollout is planned.

Polls & Emoji Sliders

Want to know more about your Instagram followers, such as what they desire, preferences, dislikes, and more? Okay, you can do it now, and it is straightforward! Recently, Instagram launched new interactive poll stickers on Instagram Stories that allows you to ask questions and see your followers "results when they vote.

The great thing about survey stickers is that it has so many market applications! Whether you want to collect feedback about your products, crowd source ideas, or entertain your followers, poll stickers offer an interesting new way to engage your Instagram target audience!

Question Stickers

Unlike emoji sliders and poll stickers, both of which allow users to "vote" questions you ask when you place a question sticker to your Instagram story; other users will submit questions for you to answer, giving them information on their queries.

Whether you are looking to collect feedback on your products or crowd source ideas, sticker questions offer an entirely new way to increase engagement with your Instagram audience!

Countdown Stickers

Now, when you post an upcoming story (such as an in-store sale, product launch, or event), you can add a ticker counting down to the date and time you set it. You can then subscribe to your countdown case, which will give you a message when the time is out, and your countdown is over!

Whether you are trying to promote a deal, a workshop, an event, or something out of the ordinary, the ability to share countdown on your stories that your followers will remember is a perfect way to deliver better results.

GIF Stickers

Instagram joined forces with GIPHY to build a high-quality GIF library on Instagram Stories in 2017. Now you can add to any photo or video in your story fun, expressive GIF stickers! It is easy to add GIFs to Instagram Stories — you will see a new GIF option when you select to add a sticker to a photo or video in stories. Click it and find a library full of hundreds of thousands of GIPHY-powered moving stickers.

Through regularly using this tool, you can add a lot of personality to your Instagram stories and help you build a loyal follower. You can get an Instagram tutorial step-by-step on how to add GIFs here to Instagram Stories.

Instagram Live Video Replays

It was not possible to replay or post Instagram Live clips after the broadcast before a recent update. And while this "restricted streaming" certainly generated a sense of urgency for people to tune in, there is a great value in being able to share your post-broadcast live clips. This new feature will make Instagram Live as big as Facebook Live!

You can post a replay of it once your Instagram Live video is done. But like other pictures and videos that you post with Instagram Stories, after 24 hours, live video replays will vanish.

Instagram Stories Highlights

Instagram Stories Highlights is an extremely valuable addition to Instagram's business profile as it allows advertisers to quickly curate and view content that consumers want to see first. Unlike the usual Instagram stories that vanish after 24 hours, Instagram Stories Highlights are curetted videos that can be grouped by subject or theme and live on your profile forever until you delete them. They appear under your bio page and above your feed for Instagram, and when someone taps them, they will play as a stand-alone story.

Post IGTV videos and Instagram posts

Did you know that IGTV and Instagram clips can also be posted in stories? Instagram Stories shared posts, or IGTV videos will show the username of the original poster, allowing users to click it to search the original post: with more and more users turning their attention to Instagram Stories, people have used stories to cross-promote their posts and IGTV videos. Now, users can easily share the post with the new re-share feature instead of including a screenshot of their feed to stories.

HOW TO USE INSTAGRAM STORIES FOR BUSINESS

Using Instagram Stories for promoting Business is now an essential part of any marketing Ad strategy for top brands in the industry. Instagram stories can help drive interaction from new and existing fans, connect with consumers, and show off your products in real-time. That said, finding ideas for Instagram Stories and deciding what to post can be difficult. Do you need inspiration?

Here are four ways for companies to use Instagram Stories:

Promoting Your Goods and Services on Instagram Stories

The Normal "tapping" success makes it a great place to create awareness for new products and services. All you need to do is fill in your story with pictures of a single product at any angle, on different people, or in different environments, and finally hit your followers with a promotion code or call-to-action.

If you can add references to your Instagram stories, it is a great place to do it.

Create a More Engaged Community

Like regular posts, if you are using Instagram Stories for company, a combination of fun, lighthearted content and promotional content is excellent for sharing. Instagram Stories is a relaxed place, so don't be afraid to post something goofy: a short video of your office pet or a picture of the post-work drinks team out there!

Run an Instagram stories takeover

An easy way to switch it to your Instagram stories is to take over an Instagram story or invite a guest to host your Instagram story. Having regular guest segments is a great way to use Instagram Stories for business to bring both variety and consistency. You can choose someone from your business team, for a "day-in-the-life" story to try it out with your own business, or you can partner with other companies in your industry to swap stories for the day. It will allow you to customize your content and keep your customers back for more.

How To Regularly Schedule Your Instagram Stories For Business

Sharing on Instagram stories is crucial to building an audience and improving your views, and you can prepare your Instagram stories just as you would organize any social posts on your content calendar. Together with your Instagram stories, organizing both your daily Instagram feed material will help keep things organized and simple.

An excellent way to get started is to build your Instagram story's fast storyboard and make sure it flows. Through describing the start, middle, and end of your plot, you will ensure that all the critical points are addressed, while still making sure that everything flows naturally.

How Instagram Stories Can Be Scheduled With Later:

1. Start by dragging and dropping your Instagram stories onto the storyboard tool, then rearrange them to fit the order you want and look like. You can also quickly resize and crop images to match the 9:16 ratio of Instagram Stories.

2. First, when it is time to post, you will add links or captions to your scheduled stories that will be copied to your phone. Through taking the time to write convincing captions and CTAs from your phone, it helps you generate more traffic and sales.

3. Next, select the time and date from the drop-down menu next to the Save Story button to schedule your Instagram Stories.

3. You will get a notification on your phone when it is time to post. And when you open the notification, it will download your stories to your phone and caption or copy links to your clipboard, making it easy to post Instagram stories in seconds.

Instagram Story's scheduling is one of the best things you can do to expand your Instagram business in 2019! It is free to use later, but to schedule posts, you'll have to upgrade to a paid plan.

Instagram Stories may have dominated how to use Instagram Live for Business 2017, but the future looks bright for live video. We suggest that you get to know the feature early if you haven"t already. While only 22 percent of companies went "online" on Instagram in 2017, 55 percent expected to use the app in 2018, according to a recent survey.

For most businesses, the idea of going "live" on Instagram is, understandably, quite daunting. Although Instagram Stories offers you the option of pre-recorded video publishing, Instagram Live does not have "retakes."

Instagram Live has recently added another feature to Instagram Live that allows users to add guests to their live streams.

The feature works by allowing people viewing a video to add someone watching the video at that time by pressing the "Add" button in the display corner. When you add an individual, he or she joins you on the monitor in a separate window below yours.

How Do You use Instagram Live For Business?

If you are hoping to achieve some of Instagram's larger marketing goals like driving sales or increasing sign-ups, it is imperative to have a strategy in place.

Instagram Live is a relaxed place, like Instagram Stories, and you can be as creative as you like! Anyway, having a solid game plan is a good idea with all that space for imagination.

The latest trend on Instagram Live

This is for companies to use the site for advertising and launch new items. And why isn't that? Creating a lot of buzz about the goods is the perfect place. Instagram Live is a great place to generate enthusiasm around your brand, whether you are announcing a new product line or hyping a future release.

Take your hottest brand and purposely reveal very few details about it to make use of this technique in your live broadcast. The mystery will frenzy your fans! Ask viewers for more information on your website after the teaser.

This method provides an aspect of exclusivity for your live video that can inspire people to act quickly, increasing the number of leads you get.

Run email set Q&As, workshops, and tutorials

There are many different formats you can adopt during your live broadcast, including Q&As, workshops, and tutorials. Each of these formats is worthwhile and bound to provide you with a lot of viewers. But if you want Instagram Live to take advantage of your company, use it as a way to collect emails.

Asking your followers to submit questions beforehand is one of the best ways to do this. You can explore this by sending your followers an email form to a landing page (share the URL of the landing page in the lead-up to your broadcast), or by including an email address that enables viewers to submit questions.

Promote your sales & campaigns.

While Instagram stories are considered "ephemeral," nothing is more fleeting than live video on Instagram. Take advantage of this by creating a sense of urgency to watch your video whenever you post them!

One of the less difficult ways to boost the audience is by providing limited-time-only deals that you will only be delivered during the show. If you have a gift, discount, advertisement, or another program you would like to give to a select few, announce it in advance! And sharing the coupon or discount code with your viewers when you go online.

INSTAGRAM INFLUENCER

When you need to get a product, and you are not sure what brand to buy from, where do you go to? Most of us visit the review sections of each product right?! Now, do you remember buying a product from store just because your favorite musician, actor, or footballer is their brand ambassador?!

Now that is the sole reason some of us buy the many products we use daily. We buy products based on word of mouth, reviews, and Influencer marketing on Instagram. Most times, the said products might not be the best available, but out five senses betray us to satisfy our love for our favorite Instagram Influencers. This is what is called Sensory Marketing utilized to promote awareness and sales of a product. Sensor marketing thrives on three major parameters-

To identify the consumer's needs and emotions

To explore and capitalize on new markets

Growing brand loyalty

Does that sound a lot like how brands use Influencers to sell various products on Instagram? Yes, you are right.

Who is an Influencer?

An Influencer is mostly described as a blogger or content creator with engaged followership on social media that shares factual information, posts and opinions on various topics, trends, products and services that interest his/her followers via social media website or a blog. As against the popular belief that an Influencer must have a large following, Influencers are so-called because of the evident engagements characterized by likes and comments on their social media accounts. In essence, lesser amount of followers translates to higher engagement rates and increased returns on investments.

Types of Influencers

Influencers come from various niches of the industry, with followings based on unique interests and contents channeled toward a specific industry. Before choosing just any Influencer, it is crucial to understand the kind of Influencer that will be relevant to you be and one that will work best to increase sales and engagements for your page as a result of their influence.

These Influencers can be categorized into four different groups, namely the nano-, micro-, macro-, and mega-Influencers.

Nano- Influencers

They have the smallest amount of followers below 10,000; however, statistics have shown that they attract the best engagements. This is because; brands believe they are more cost-effective to manage in terms of payment than the mega Influencers. Also, they generate high engagement rates and a more significant ROI for potential brands.

Consumers love them because; they give recommendations easily and also respond to their questions, which promotes the Influencer"s brand as authentic and transparent. Consumers see the nano-Influencers as more genuine compared to the stars with mega-Influencer status, who they believe to be a simple digital marketing tactic.

Micro-Influencers

They have less than 100,000 followers, and they are mostly seen as experts in whatever field they find themselves. Just like the nano- Influencers, they produce high ROI for brands, but they are not cheaper when compared with the nano-Influencers. The audience of a micro-Influencer is targeted to a particular niche; they give brands an easier route to tap into the market.

Macro-Influencers

They have followers ranging from above 100,000 to below one million. They may be celebrities or micro-Influencers who have diligently grown their followership base. In such a case, they take Instagram Influencer marketing as a full-time job.

Mega-Influencers

They have above one million followers and are usually prominent celebrities.

What is Influencer marketing?

Influencer marketing involves partnering with an Influencer, as a content marketing strategy to promote your brand, products, and services within an agreed time frame. Influencer marketing could be via sponsored blog posts (affiliate marketing system), sponsored Instagram posts and stories, sponsored offline events with an Influencer appearance (for example, at conferences, store openings, meet and greet, and panel workshops), and other sponsored social media marketing posts. Your reason for wanting an Instagram Influencer should be unique to your brand statements. Some people target Influencers to boost an increase in their coverage, brand awareness and some to increase conversion. However, statistics have proven that most brands employ the partnerships of Influencers to raise brand awareness.

Instagram and Influencer Marketing

Instagram is becoming a fast-growing social media channel with more than one billion active users monthly; it is no surprise the market for Instagram Influencers is growing because you need the influence to stay relevant amidst the millions of active users daily.

Although the platform is still second to Facebook in terms of engagement, the millennials" are championing the events on Instagram. Active Instagram users are young people raging between 24- 34 years, and they constitute about 70% of the active user base. This means that Influencers would leverage this information to promote brand-led communications, including marketing campaigns, polls and keep an average user connected to the brands.

The Benefits of using Instagram as your Influencer marketing Platform

The searches for "Influencer marketing" on Google have grown by a whopping 1500% in 3years, and you can bet there is a good reason for such. This is because brands, individuals and Influencers alike are beginning to see they are useful to the system and Influencers can create buzz off the slightest events which is good publicity for any brand. Here's why!

Builds organic traffic

One of the exciting reasons people love Instagram is due to the traffic it drives. Influencer marketing is a thing today due to the strong organic driving force of traffic it generates. It features real-time content in form of pictures and videos appealing to the emotions of consumers to patronize the various brands they are influencing.

These high-quality posts provide easy access for consumers to have engagements with an Influencer. Rather than staying stuck to whatever brand consumers are exposed to, Instagram offers consumers content they can resonate with to promote active engagements.

This means Influencers have the liberty to represent your brand as brand ambassadors, use their creativity to include your products and services into their daily lives and showcasing it on Instagram In the best way possible to their large number of followers who will resonate with your brand to drive organic traffic and active engagements.

The Niche

Instagram is created in a way that it provides various channels via which consumers can discover the niche they are interested in with ease. There is the use of hashtags, which gathers all information concerning that singular hashtag used by different people in one location and gives you thousands of choices to choose from.

Many leading brands have also created their hashtags, which they use for campaigns and brand awareness and even encourage their followers to use it to increase traffic and awareness on their pages.

There is also the Instagram explore page that is specially designed for each user based on the people you follow and the content you resonate with. You can also check out the channels feature which explores pages based on niches such as travel, sports, fashion and lots more. And lastly on selecting a niche, is the Instagram Algorithm, though it changes daily, is designed to show users' contents they are more likely to engage in. It helps to boost posts from an account a user frequently engages in. In all these, it gives you an ample choice to find a great niche you might be interested in since thousands of Influencers might also be interested in that niche.

It's Personal

One of the most significant reasons Instagram Influencer marketing thrives better than most means of advertisement is due to the connection between the Influencers and their target audience, which becomes a personal platform for most people to "tell it as it is."

The best way to be successful in influencer marketing is to leverage on an authentic, genuine, and informed relationship with your followers. By having using Influencers as brand ambassadors on Instagram, their followers would perceive your brand as reliable, trustworthy, and a successful one that will deliver on it is promises. These Influencers engage their followers with different posts, encouraging them to shop with your brand.

Attributes to look out for in an Influencer

Whatever social marketing strategy you decide to use for your brands, products and services need a strategic approach. There a lot more to selecting the right people for your Instagram campaign than selecting an Influencer with a large following or what Influencer marketing agency they work with. So, in this book, I have outlined, the qualities and Instagram metrics you should consider when looking for the most suitable influencer for your brand.

Brand fit.

Looking for the perfect brand fit goes a long way to determine the success of an Instagram Influencer marketing campaign. Let's say you sell natural hair products, you would require an Instagram Influencer who's got thick and long natural hair and would give out tips on how to grow hair of such length and thickness and how to avoid the pitfalls.

By discovering the perfect Influencer fit for your brand, your Influencer partnership will look more authentic and trusted from a consumer's perspective and in turn, will add more ROI potential to your campaign and generate leads for your business.

Below are a few ways you can search out the perfect brand fit with a potential influencer

Find the niche they fall into by looking at Influencers" recent posts and stories.

Find out what conversations spark from the Influencer's content by looking at the comments section.

Engagement rate.

Gone are those times when a huge number of followers would determine how to pick the perfect Influencer fit for your brand; these days, the rate and measurement of engagements have become top priority for big brands.

Follower count has ceased to be the measurement to scope out Influencers. Most recently, the need to measure engagement rate has become top of mind and increasingly crucial to brands. This is very important because it over the years some of these Influencers have mastered the art of buying fake followers to maintain their status in the social media space.

Although, as at this time of writing this book, there are no tangible ways of determining how to identify fake followers, hence the need to monitor the engagement rates in the comment section of the Influencer you want to partner with. Engagement rate can be measured by the number of likes, shares and comments per post divided by the total number of followers of that Influencer. Like it was earlier stated, the nano and micro Influencers have the highest engagement rates, and that should be the first group to look for your ideal Influencer for your brand. Yeah, the celebrities have their influence too, but the Influencers with a target audience that will generate revenue and increase your ROI are the micro and nano-Influencers.

Past sponsors

Before deciding to partner with an Influencer, research to find out the people they have partnered with in the past. Find out if they are your competitors or brands that will compliment your product. By carrying out this study, you will discover how such campaigns have performed in the past and see how your partnership with the Influencer would look like in the long run. This would give you an informed decision for your marketing plan.

Clear communication.

Nobody likes to be kept waiting, and the same law applies to social media marketing. Consider how quickly these Influencers respond and do they give detailed response or act snobbish? Because this will tell how people would perceive your brand in the long run.

Between creating quality and quick response, clear communication is vital to the success of an Instagram Influencer marketing campaign, so ensure you can rely on the line of communication from a potential Influencer.

Love for your brand.

Influencers thrive on the authenticity of their brand. Do you think the Influencer would be interested in your brand based on their timeline? Can they promote your brand without sponsorship? Do you trust them to publish genuine promotions of your brand, or is it just another source of income for them?

Answer these questions, and they would give you an informed idea of the best Influencer fit for your brand. All in all, ensure you select an Influencer that will advertise your brand with so much creativity, excitement and authenticity.

How Do You Compensate These Influencers?

As a brand, you can compensate Influencers in three ways:

- With free products,
- Rates that work based on their marketing budget
- Commission from the use of affiliates.

There is no perfect way to determine the best compensation type for an Influencer; it is usually based on the agreement you have with the person. And you may need to take into account the audience your Influencer will be addressing, the performance metrics with which you plan to measure your progress and their content creation and delivery.

When determining the amount to compensate an Influencer, you will need to take into account the following aspects:

Production (e.g. the duration of the ad and what will be required to create the post).

Travel expenses (e.g. for travel Influencers, this includes factors like airline and hotel fees).

Agency fees (this is more prevalent for macro- and mega-Influencers).

Additional usage rights (e.g. exclusivity requirements, other images for brand use, paid media requests, and white labelling content).

Choosing the type of payment or compensation plan for Influencers is not a straight call. It has to be hinged on the campaign at hand, what you expect in return in terms of brand awareness; and the Influencer's metrics and brand fit.

The Three Types of Payment/compensation for Influencers

Free products

In this case, the Influencer is given complimentary free products or services that can be used by the Influencer; for example a cosmetic brand can provide an Influencer with a range of their products such as body creams and bath soaps.

Paid Compensation

Here, the brand pays the Influencer a stipulated amount to promote their brand for an agreed period based on the rates from the Influencers and the marketing budget of the brand.

Affiliate compensation

In this case, an Influencer gets commission via the use of affiliate links from different platforms the brand is linked to. Some brands use a double payment system by adding paid compensation to affiliate compensation.

How do you decide what payment plan to pursue? Here are a few strategies to help you make the best decision-

Instances where you can compensate with Free Product:

The Influencer is an existing customer.

The Influencer is still new in the business with a small engagement rating, with minimal signs of social engagements.

The Influencer is more interested in the impact you make and how it will boost his/her "Influencer brand" (e.g. non-profit campaign).

When to Compensate with Dollars:

The Influencer's livelihood is by making money on Instagram

The Influencer has a large fan base with clear signs of engagements

The Influencer has laid down rates and prices.

Payment by Instagram Content Medium

Prices differ for each category, and there is no perfect price estimation even within each medium.

Be sure to set a target ROI metric when negotiating prices. Let's assume that your goal is to increase reach–then set a metric-based level of reach or impression with that influencer. This will help manage expenses and keep the brand-Influencer relationship consistent with the campaign's goals.

Instagram stories

They could cost from a few bucks to a few hundred dollars everywhere. For obvious reasons, Instagram Stories are the cheapest medium–they're a new type of content, they're brief, need less effort to create, and they're quick content bits! While there are different rates for each post, as part of a package deal, most influencers have Instagram Stories.

Picture Posts

Instagram posts featuring your business, product or service are a mid-range cost that can start about $150-$300 for nano-and micro-influencer–and add up to (hundreds of) thousands of dollars for macro-or mega-influencers.

Video Posts

There's no doubt that for both your product and the influencer, clips take longer to produce –that means you should expect a heftier price tag. These can cost up to $500 with the fee of the influencer and the purchase of goods inclusive.

Where can I find Influencers?

All great ways to recruit potential influencers are self-discovery, influencer companies and influencer networks. You can use a specific method to source your Influencers depending on the resources of your company.

Here are some of the best Instagram Influencers source locations. Scroll down Instagram. Yeah, it can be that easy!

Scroll through Instagram and pick influencers that you feel will suit your campaign well. While sending them an Instagram Direct Message is simple, in their profile biography, you can find their contact information.

1. RewardStyle.

RewardStyle is recognized as the world's leading forum for influencer marketing monetization. Through offering end-to-end influencer solutions, the business makes it easy for brands to thrive. Working with rewardStyle is an excellent choice for brands seeking to increase sales through Influencer marketing thanks to their leading Influencer marketing shopping app.

2.LIKEtoKNOW.IT.

LIKEtoKNOW.IT enables Instagram users to screenshot posts from their favorite influencers and to shop the related items in the program. Then, through their ties, influencers earn a commission for purchased items. This is what you can expect from rewardStyle from a company perspective:

• Full-service Influencer services.

• Organic sales and contents that can be tracked.

• Licensing of content.

• Integration of meetings and events.

• Improved distribution.

• Consulting for production.

3. AspireIQ.

AspireIQ, listed by Forrester as a pioneer in Influencer marketing strategies, provides marketers with the following:

• Identification of influencer.

- Identification of influencers.

- Review of the campaign.

- Scaling relationships with the influencer.

The unique aspect of AspireIQ is that to find the most relevant influencers for your brand, the company uses AI-driven software to analyze millions of influencer comments. This can save time (and money) for you!

4. Traackr.

Through their IRM–Influencer Relationship Management Model, Traackr prides itself on helping marketers transform their Influencer marketing strategies.

Here's what Traackr might offer:

- Exploring different influencers.

- Assessment of influencer (yes –also monitoring how many true followers somebody has).

- Insights of the audience.

- Planning and management of campaigns.

- Visibility and communication.

- Safety of the company.

- Quality of predictive influencer.

- Analysis of observations and patterns.
- Measurement of cross campaigns.

5. Collectively.

Influencer marketing platforms take a different approach collectively. The company, calling itself an influencer marketing agency, is putting itself in a spot for change–recognizing that channels of influencer will change with time.

Collectively, you can find the following services:

Start tracking for Your Next Influencer Campaign.

When you set up and run your Influencer Campaign, you need to know how it went. Do not just look at statistics when assessing the campaign–but the real relationship between your company and the influencer. And yes –influencers are also doing this with their business!

This will give you the full range for the campaign's success. However, the exercise may even help you identify areas for potential development.

The Metrics

Here are some examples of online metrics that you should measure during an Influencer marketing campaign. Keep in mind that the metrics can vary depending on the campaign's goals.

- Commitment to the outcomes of the campaign.

- Brand feeling: (how people talk about your brand?)

- Referral traffic (shows many visitors came to your page from the campaign?)

- Sales (conversions and revenue generated)

- Follower count (had it improved significantly?) Influencer relationship evaluation Just as crucial as data evaluation, take a few moments to evaluate the relationship. Here are few suggestions of what to think and look for.

- Has the influencer ever met with the deadlines?

- Have they met the specifications of the content?

Are they going beyond and beyond supporting their followers " content?

- Shared some feedback? (e.g. wanting to work together again in the future)

If you consider your relationship to be fruitful and constructive, make sure that you want to encourage the partnership in the future.

Note–After a campaign, influencers often assess their product relationship, so make sure you do your part too!

HOW TO LEVERAGE ON INSTAGRAM INFLUENCERS

These days, there are more and more products and service brands, daily turning to social media to increase their reach to their potential customers. In a world where social interaction is fast becoming the fastest way to close a deal, your business would do better with an influencer boosting your engagements as a result of their followers, engagement and the traffic they help generate. The main goal of Instagram influencers is to spread the word, create awareness and increase sales!

Everyone in the business world has started to work with influencers to attract more clients and improve their ROI. According to reports by Tomlinson, it was reported that not only is influencer marketing cost-effective, but it is also the fastest-growing customer acquisition channel and more than 51%of marketers claim they have reached out to a large number of potential customers with the use of influencers and in this case Instagram Influencers.

That being said, the easier part is to know that you need an influencer for your brand, the harder question is how do you leverage on this opportunity? How do you create a long-lasting, hassle-free and productive partnership with an influencer? This chapter aims to answer your questions and throw more light on how you can maximize your collaboration with an Instagram influencer.

In the previous chapter, we discussed defining your niche and how and where to attract an influencer and the mode of compensation.

Leveraging deals with how effectively you utilize the given opportunity to your business advantage. Now that you have found an influencer that may be interested in your niche, how do you work your magic to get them involved in your business?

Reach out to the influencer in a calm but direct manner.

The first thing to do is to send a message to the influencer in a professional and non-aggressive manner not to start stalking and liking and retweeting all their posts from 2014! I mean, where have you been all their lives?! That is creepy for a start, mainly because nobody likes a stalker!

The most important point to bear in mind is that you don't want to sloppily start messaging, retweeting, and sharing every one of your target influencers' posts. When they see you've "liked" 25 of their Instagram posts from 2015, they are more likely to freak out rather than being flattered.

Instead, make your message as courteous and straightforward as possible. And while you are reaching out to them devise a strategic plan that you propose to share with the influencer on what you would like to achieve with the partnership. Allow the Influencer time to respond, do not send repeated messages like an overly eager person representing your brand.

Join online chats where your influencer is active

Another way to reach out to your Ideal influencer is to check the media circles and see where this influencer participates in, what topic interests him/her the people they follow, and so on. it could even be a social hangout. There has to be a social hangout where they actively participate in, that's what makes them an influencer. So whether it is on Twitter, Instagram, LinkedIn, and Facebook; keep searching till you find where they are active, hang out there and get involved in the chats; dropping intelligent remarks, so you don't come off as unserious.

Here's an example – Twitter is a great place to make your existence known to your social media influencers. There are conversations on Twitter that occur almost every week, and your influencer might be involved in it, use a common hashtag to find these trends and join in. The fantastic thing about using this strategy is that you can join these hashtag conversations, lightly participate in them as regularly as they hold them, and with time, your social media influencer targets will start recognizing your Twitter handle.

Then, when you do reach out to them for an influencer-brand partnership, it won't feel random, and your target social influencer will be much more likely to respond. If you are conversant with twitter trends, you will discover that there are various Twitter chats and trends for every industry, join one today and don't a stranger!

It Doesn't Hurt To Make A Human Connection

Nothing beats making a real-life connection to strike a deal; it allows you to take your time to explain what and how you want to achieve it. You might be thinking, social media business should stay on social media, but human interaction breaks a lot of boundaries, and you might even get luckier to striking a better deal. Whether you like it or not, research has shown that communicating in person is much more impactful than online communication.

So, should you turn up at the door of your influencer with a 65-slide PowerPoint presentation about how you could work together? No, not! They would get bored! Alternatively, if your influencer is local, keep an eye on their social media feeds to see the social events they tweet about. Register for the same events, attend and try to make a natural human connection.

Ensure you enter the venue very prepared with the idea you want to pitch but also listen to what your influencer is saying to get more knowledge even if it means listening to how much they love themselves and what they have achieved; just enjoy the ride, afterward you are at the event already, so you should make the most of it.

Bear in mind that your initial conversation should be light and exchange contacts and connect on social media if you haven't already so that you can reach out to them later. At least you won't be a stranger anymore. This tip is great because you have an 89%chance of getting a good response the next time you reach out to the influencer.

Leverage Your Network

Use your inner circle network to get the necessary connections and links you need to meet your social media influencer. Ask your friends; someone must know the gateway to your influencer. The same zeal you apply when looking for a job should be the same zeal you should use when trying to reach your influencer. This may seem very challenging, but search through your social media influencer's friends to find out if you have a mutual connection; you might be surprised that the world is smaller than you think. Reach out to this mutual friend to know if they are connected, and you can plan a meeting with the influencer, with your friend making the introductions. This will ensure your potential influencer doesn't get caught off-guard by a miscellaneous reach-out.

HOW TO UTILIZE INSTAGRAM WITH YOUR DIRECT SALES BUSINESS

At this point, you no uncertainty will have known about the famous photo tool Instagram. This is an app accessible for cell phones that enables clients to add special visualizations to their photos before sharing them through social media. As of late, Instagram has likewise developed as a valuable business engagement tool. It has brilliant computerized PR potential, so here are five different ways brands can utilize the app to build engagement.

Photo competitions

One great choice for brands utilizing Instagram is to hold photo competitions and encourage clients to enter. The app is easy to utilize and a lot of people approach it, so all there's chances you'll get a decent reaction - particularly if there is an alluring prize on offer for the victor. This kind of competition can likewise lead to greater introduction, particularly if contestants share their photos all alone social media pages.

Brand marketing

Organizations can likewise utilize Instagram pictures for their brand marketing. For instance, just as drawing in a SEO agency to make sure a brand can be found in search motor outcomes, a company could add additional appeal to their marketing with eye-getting Instagram images of products. These can be integrated into a social media strategy so as to encourage engagement.

Occasion advancement

Another approach to encourage engagement utilizing Instagram is to tackle people control around upcoming occasions. By connecting to pre-characterized and branded hashtags organizations can welcome clients to upload their own photos of the occasion along with the applicable hashtag in this manner touching off discussion among your intended interest groups.

Client photos

Toward the start of 2012, Instagram had 15 million clients. Presently it has 50 million. This fast growth, in addition to the way that numerous people love to share photos through social media, means that you can undoubtedly find social media clients who additionally use Instagram. Sharing cool client photos on Facebook and Twitter can be a decent path for brands to draw in with new people and tell them that they're appreciated. For instance, just as running the more traditional photo competitions talked about above, you could get people to send in their favorite pictures on the understanding that you'll share the best - giving your clients attention just as advancing your brand.

In the background information

At last, a few brands are additionally utilizing Instagram to share in the background photos of their workplaces to give people more knowledge into what they do and help spread a progressively human picture of their brand.

A growing number of social media organizations are utilizing Instagram to promote their brand, as it's unquestionably worth looking at it to perceive what the app could accomplish for your company.

Streamlining your Instagram channel for direct sales will lead to huge prizes. By overlooking the essentials of marketing on Instagram, you enable the competition to succeed.

Marketing on Instagram increases your website traffic and the number of prospect every month. Truly, Instagram is only that incredible!

Underneath I give you the top tips for all affiliate advertisers. If that you are attempting to sell your direct sales products utilizing Instagram you have to continue reading.

1: Tell People What to Do

Nothing will grow your business rapidly than telling your audience what exactly you want them to do. This is a Call to Action. It works, it is time tried, and it is valid. In the quick paced universe of social media, you should show your audience how you can support them. At that point you immediately reveal to them where to go for that help. Truth be told you audience will appreciate the "directly to the point" strategy.

From our direct understanding, Instagram is a unique social media divert in this regard. A random individual on Instagram will to take a gander at an image, check the portrayal, and pursue the source of inspiration. Straightforward as that. To acquire sales on Instagram you should give a source of inspiration "Click the link in profile in the event that you need to learn more!"

For a fact, when the source of inspiration goes before the stunning offer you get more leads.

Sounds stunning right? Well prepare to be blown away. It works.

There are numerous approaches to lure your audience. Everything begins with putting the correct and appropriate pictures and suggestions to take action out there. This leads to tip #2.

2. Recognize Your Audience's Preference

Pictures that appeal to the client's inclination is the most significant advance for bringing your business on Instagram.

Finding, focusing on, and remaining important to your audience is the basic factor. Also, regardless of whether you make the most salary from this platform.

Recognizing your audience's inclination is an immense theme. I have seen what it leads to when business proprietors post an inappropriate content to the ideal audience. Allows simply state it isn't beautiful!

Fortunately, you are reading this with some understanding of your audience's inclinations. So this ought to be basic. Investigate carefuuly your Instagram feed and look at the popular posts. What has gotten remarks, offers and likes? Your audience will have similar tastes and inclinations you do. Start each Instagram post with the inquiry "Would this picture arouse my advantage?" "Would I purchase this?" If you answer truly, at that point you have discovered great content.

Think about heading off to some of your rival's pages too. Look at their popular posts and pictures. As you find pictures your niche audience is communicating with, make comparable ones for your page.

When you've set up your audience's inclinations, the time has come to move onto tip #3.

3 Identify the Profit Points/location

Your adaptation choices and options on Instagram remain constrained when you speak to a direct sales company. Most direct sales organizations don't enable their affiliates to take out advertising space. Read the fine print on your affiliate participation. Chances are great that paid advertising isn't permitted.

So what are you supposed to do?

Do you remember tip #1? The source of inspiration? Your affiliate circumstance requests that you utilize a ground-breaking source of inspiration to a profit location.

Be that as it may, pause. Try not to post your affiliate link in this location, create an interesting freebie instead. You will probably lead the audience to content. You can then post this freebie link on Instagram and any social network. This link will gather email leads from people who need more information.

What is content? Content is information your niche audience needs. If you speak to the make-up industry, at that point perhaps a freebie on the best way to form is a decent alternative. If you speak to the wellbeing and health industry, at that point low fat plans would work.

The reason for these profit locations is to take your Instagram audience and transform them into leads. Give a source of inspiration to "Click the Link in the Profile" in the depiction. This is your profit location. Next you move from the profit point/location to a sales channel. Continue reading for tip #4.

4: Educate, Give Variety and Repeat

After you have driven your audience to the profit location you have to have a strategy. Take the leads who needed your freebie and transform them into a product sale.

We recommend an approach that utilizations three distinct features.

Start with instruction.

A lead who needs your freebie is a "freebie-searcher'. Until you catch up with instruction about your important products they will never purchase.

Provide them with the information they need and start building trust.

Give your leads assortment.

A basic of spanning the lead into a sale is to have a multistep follow-up succession set up. Create a marketing plan that considers email marketing, limits, and important "how to" illustrations. Consider infographics that show them another method with your products. Assortment likewise means including solicitations to online classes or other live occasions facilitated by you. This is the way to seeing them through to the sale, what works for certain people won't work for other people. You should have enough assortment to catch sales from a wide range of characters.

Reiteration.

People need to hear a similar message a normal of 12 times before it at last kicks in. You may feel depleted at rehashing your information about your products again and again. Understandable. Yet, you should understand that your customers didn't hear you the first time. They have not heard you the second or third or fourth time!

Don't make the mix-up of reasoning your one "previously, then after the fact" picture on Instagram will get you a sale. The reason for Instagram marketing leads the possibility into a sales domain. It is here where you communicate with them again and again. In the event that your audience heard the sales pitch the first time, you would have already had a great many sales.

Since that isn't the situation, at that point chances are, they have not heard your pitch. Remove them from the social media channel with a source of inspiration. Direct them to a 'profit location'. Set up a variable marketing campaign and converse with them once more, and once more, and once more.

5 Analysis and Optimization

At long last, analysis and advancement must be an enormous part of your Instagram strategy. There are two diverse analysis systems you have to understand. Quantitative (measurement) and Qualitative (non-measurement).

Quantitative

This is the place you can quantify and measure the engagement with each picture/post. Create (or utilize an analysis app) where you can figure the collaboration from each post.

Your ideal measurement will be the quantity of clicks to your link in profile.

You will need to measure what number of those clicks changed over to a lead (they gave you an email). Quantitative measurement shows you income potential. At the point when every one of those leads uses your marketing campaign (tip #4) you have a decent starting point.

You will probably make compelling Instagram campaigns. So the more the information you can add to this analysis, the more powerful you'll be.

• Day/time of day posted

• Content sort - link, photo, video and so on.

• Ratio of link clicks to lead catches.

Utilize this strategy to build an image of which endeavors are profitable, and which are an exercise in futility.

Qualitative

Qualitative analysis is taking a gander at the parts of your marketing that isn't numbers. Your qualitative analysis will cover the objectives of your business. Here are a few inquiries to begin with.

• Am I giving enough information? Does my content support my endeavors (giving people enough source of inspiration's)?

- Does my freebie link perform well for the Instagram platform?

- Given all that I think about marketing, do I seem to be a "spammer"?

- Am I offering real incentive to my intended interest group?

These qualitative measurements ought to be one of the most significant contemplations. Is it true that you are paying enough consideration regarding the administration that you offer or would you say you are simply attempting to make a buck? Trust us. People know the distinction between a sales individual and somebody who leads with esteem.

The main way you will make sales is by being the worth leader first through qualitative analysis. The more worth you give away the more achievement you will understanding.

This procedure is a long one.

It might feel safe to forcefully promote your direct sales products on social media. Once more, trust us. Set aside the effort to speak to yourself as the worth leader and you will acquire greater profit over the long haul.

Conclusion

You have read 5 hints to adapt your direct sales business utilizing Instagram.

1. Instruct people

2. Recognize your audience's inclinations

3. Recognize the profit location

4. Teach, assortment, and redundancy

5. Analysis and advancement

Make use of these means and you will be head and shoulders over your industry competition. Direct sales is profitable on social media. In any case, you must demonstrate that you are advantageous to your audience first.

INFLUENCER MARKETING DEFINED?

Influencer marketing is a form of joint effort. A business collaborates with a persuasive individual to promote something. It could be a product, administration, or campaign. Celebrity supports were the first form of influencer marketing. Yet, in today's computerized world, social content makers with niche audiences can regularly offer more an incentive to brands. These people have committed and drawn in groups of followers via web-based networking media. They are referred to just as "web based life influencers." More than 66% of North American retailers utilize some form of influencer marketing. What's more, practically 50% of US and UK computerized advertisers spend in any event 10% of their marketing correspondence budget on influencer marketing.

Not persuaded influencer marketing can lead to genuine business results? A study found that 34% of every day U.S. Instagram clients purchased something in light of the fact that a blogger or influencer suggested it. Instagram is the platform of decision for social influencers. 89% of advertisers distinguish it as one of the most significant channels for influencer marketing. About 33% of the influencer content on Instagram appears in Stories. This number will probably grow this year. The swipe-up feature to link out from Instagram Stories is presently accessible to accounts with only 10,000 followers. This makes Stories a great spot to share and link to brand content. Yet, don't disregard different platforms. About a fourth of day by day Facebook clients have made a buy based on a blogger or influencer suggestion. So have 29% of day by day Twitter clients.

How to find the right social media influencer in 8 easy steps

There are in excess of 500,000 dynamic influencers on Instagram alone. That means you have numerous potential open doors for influencer joint effort. It additionally means you need to place in the work to find the privilege influencer. Advertisers' trust in their capacity to find the privilege influencer changes generally by nation. In China, 81% of marketing experts are certain they can find effective influencers. In the United States, just 39% of advertisers feel a similar way.

Here are 8 key approaches to find and associate with the privilege influencer for your campaign.

1. Think about the three Rs of influence

Influence is made up of three parts:

- Relevance
- Reach
- Resonance

Relevance

An applicable influencer shares content important to your business and industry. They have to have an audience that lines up with your objective market. For instance, Intrepid Travel worked with a group of vegetarian influencers to dispatch its new veggie lover visits. The influencers' had an exceptionally significant audience that the company accessed in a drawing in and authentic way. Erin Ireland is an energetic veggie lover advocate. Her Instagram post about how the visit opened up movement for her in India as a vegetarian increased in excess of 5,700 preferences.

Reach

Reach is the quantity of people you might reach through the influencer's devotee base.

Resonance

This is the potential degree of engagement the influencer can create with an audience pertinent to your brand. Greater isn't in every case better. A colossal adherent tally is insignificant if those followers aren't keen on your offer. What's more, a littler supporter check can be ground-breaking if it's a niche zone. Niche influencers can have exceptionally devoted and connected with followers. Tapinfluence found that engagement rates are frequently higher for "micro-influencers." Micro-influencers have 5,000 to 25,000 followers. 30% of North American retailers presently work with micro-influencers. The most recent improvement is the development of nano-influencers. These influencers can have as not many as 1,000 followers, yet their statement is gold to their committed fans.

2. Be sure of who you're attempting to influence

Your influencer campaign can't be everything to all people. A practical strategy anticipates that you should address the ideal people using the right tools. (Likewise, for this circumstance, the benefit influencers).The introductory advance is to describe who your audience will be for this particular campaign. Making audience personas is a great technique to make sure you understand who you're attempting to reach. At the point when you've done that, create a planning arrangement of influencer personas. This will help you with understanding the attributes you're searching for in your influencers.

3. Search for engagement and trust with the right audience

The key is trust. Your audience must trust and respect the evaluation of the influencers you partner with. Without the trust portion, any results will be superficial. You'll fight to see a significant business influence from your undertakings. How might you tell if your potential influencer is trusted? Engagement. You have to see a lot of viewpoints, likes, comments, and offers. In particular, you have to see these from the definite adherent areas you're attempting to reach. A not too bad engagement rate additionally means a dedicated after, instead of an inflated adherent check fortified by bots and coercion accounts.

4. Go for a reliable look, feel, tone, and qualities

You have to find somebody who's creating content with a look and feel that supplements your own. The tone should likewise be appropriate for the manner in which you need to introduce your brand to potential customers. This will guarantee things don't feel disconnected in either party's internet based life posts.

5. Watch out for sponsorship immersion

Investigate the post of your potential influencers from time to time. How regularly would they say they are sharing sponsored content? If they're already hitting followers with huge amounts of paid posts, their engagement rate may not last. Search for a lot of natural, non-paid content to keep followers intrigued, excited, and locked in. YouTube influencer Laura Reid prescribes just having one in each five or 10 posts sponsored. Remember this when considering what you'll ask the influencer to post, also. Requesting an excessive number of posts in a short timeframe will make your offer hard for the influencer to acknowledge, regardless of whether it accompanies an enormous paycheck.

6. Research and learn

Popular influencers get lots of offers. At the point when you first approach an influencer, you'll have to show that you've placed in the time to learn what they do. Get to recognizes what their channels are about and who their audience is. Shockingly better, start your approach gradually by collaborating naturally with your objective influencer's posts. Like their content. Remark when appropriate. Be appreciative, not salesly.

7. Plan your budget

Influencers with broad reach appropriately hope to be paid for their work. Free product may work with nano-influencers, yet a bigger influencer campaign requires a budget. Consider what sort of payment structure makes the most sense for your goals. Be that as it may, be happy to think about the influencer's needs, as well. For instance, an affiliate or commission structure may be a choice instead of a flat fee, or to lessen the flat fee. We've sketched out the different payment models in our post on the most proficient method to pay Instagram influencers. Remember that micro-influencers and nano-influencers will have increasingly adaptable payment terms.

8. Reach out personally, and privately

An immediate message is a great spot to start. In the event that you can find an email address, attempt that as well. However, don't send a mass email or conventional DM. It might take somewhat longer to compose an individual message to each influencer. In any case, it will show you're not kidding about a potential partnership. This will thusly build your chances of striking an arrangement.

How to Get Instagram Sponsorship for Making Money

When you clock 1000 plus followers on Instagram and on the look for sponsorship in Instagram, do you know how to proceed? If the uncertainty factor in Instagram sponsorship is weighing heavily on your heart, then don't fret.It is likely to get Instagram sponsorship for small accounts and garner more exposure in your niche market by making excellent and engaging videos. In this section, we are going to introduce the ways that would help you get sponsorship in Instagram and earn more revenues.

- Part1: Is it possible to find Instagram sponsorship for small accounts
- Part2: How to get Instagram sponsorship

Part 1: Is it possible to find Instagram sponsorship for small accounts

Gone are the days when brands only looked for extremely popular influencers with a trailing list of followers. Under their Instagram sponsorship program now brands look for micro-influencers within the exact niche. Because they shed less bucks to reach the right audience in a target demographics. Micro-influencers are low-budget but high rewards aspects for any business. Usually Instagram popular accounts are less interactive, when compared to average Instagram accounts from the ROI point of view. There is less engagement for accounts having millions of followers. When you have a limited number of followers, your response will be instant and the engagement will be better. Instagram sponsored posts nowadays come with brand + influencer collaborations. This is an integral part for your business to flourish in Instagram.

Part 2: How to get Instagram sponsorship

1. Know your audience well

Understanding what content on your Instagram posts satisfies your audience isn't sufficient. You have to dive further and become acquainted with how to make your posts associate with them better with your product or services. Step by step instructions to bring out their feelings based on their age range, area, sexual orientation conveyance, and how did your post performed. Instagram sponsorship would turn out to be easy, when you will obviously clarify brands about your followers' needs and likes. Realizing that you have better understanding about the niche and sort of audience will score more atta boy with the brands ready to collaborate with you.

2. Use Instagram sponsorship apps

There are various apps that assist you with working together with advertisers and influencers to promote your brand. Influencer platforms advance your name in the influencer shopping commercial center, accordingly the brand sponsorships crosswise over significant online networking platforms start seeing you. GOsnap is one of the best assistance with leading influencers on Instagram, Twitter, and YouTube. On the off chance that you get a chance, don't stop for a second to collaborate with your favorite brands for paid Instagram sponsorship. GOsnap offers you easy signup with your internet based life account, no agreements to sign, paid sponsorship bargains directly at your versatile, join campaigns that you love and so forth in addition, share visit individual posts via web-based networking media with followers and acquire more bucks through ledger or PayPal.

3. Contact the brand you like

Connect with your favorite brands decisively to pitch your thought. You can likewise label their brand name, account or handle with your post. With an influencer's content thought, you get significant and authentic sponsorship for your Instagram posts.

4. Improve engagement rate.

Expanded engagement on your Instagram posts means better change to get featured on the Instagram Explore page. This page on Instagram permits influencers reach people who are not their followers .A snappy viral status over yonder could be the what tops off an already good thing for you. With the correct content and adhering to the fundamental Instagram rules would soar your chances of better presentation. Peruse your adherent's page and remark on their posts. Join Instagram remarks units for better informing with your followers to upgrade the engagement.

5. Be genuine and authentic

Instagram sponsorship programs expect you to be authentic and reasonable. Continuously make sure to remain consistent with your followers and post content that is speaking to your brand identity. While working together with brands and influencers on Instagram acquires more incomes. Never, disregard the way that your followers are the purpose for your growth. Instead of clustering your account with posts that are unmistakable difference to your brand identity would cost you losing your followers, pick the ones that hold your visual identity. While you give a whoop to different brands, don't lose your brand's voice by any stretch of the imagination.

6. Don't neglect to affiliate

Instagram sponsorship for little accounts is clearly going to assist you with pushing forward. Along with that, be sure to affiliate with others for upgrading the sales of your brand's products or services. An affiliate is essentially engaged at improving the sales of brands partnering with them for a commissions. Though influencers are essentially associated with making brand awareness. There is an identifiable link or certain promotion code that followers can click for really purchasing your administration/product. As links in Instagram are permitted distinctly in the bio, you need to think of one as product on the double for applying affiliate links. Making promotion codes is a superior substitute to lace them with your posts. However, Instagram is permitting links in Instagram Stories now.

Here are some famous affiliate platforms with online shippers that you can investigate – ClickBank, RewardStyle, and Amazon's Affiliate Program are not many of them. Utilize other marketing channels and your website to reinforce the affiliate program.

GUIDE TO CREATING INSTGRAM ADS

What Is Instagram Advertising?

Instagram advertising is strategy for paying to post sponsored content on the Instagram platform to reach a bigger and more focused on audience. While there are many reasons a business or individual may choose to advertise, Instagram advertising is frequently used to grow brand introduction, website traffic, generate new leads, and move current leads down the pipe (and hopefully towards converting).Since Instagram is such a visual platform, content ads are not a thing here. Or maybe you need a picture, set of pictures, or video (which can be joined by content) to reach your audience with Instagram ads. The energizing part? Instagram advertising works! In March 2017, more than 120 million Instagrammers visited a website, got headings, called, messaged, or direct informed to find out about a business based on an Instagram advertisement. As indicated by Instagram, 60% of people say they find new products on the platform, and 75% of Instagrammers make a move subsequent to being enlivened by a post. Like Facebook ads, tossing some cash behind a post will prompt more introduction for your brand, just as more authority over who can see your post.

The amount Do Instagram Ads Cost?

This is a dubious inquiry to reply, as costs are based on an assortment of factors, and as you may have suspected these factors are not all uncovered to us by the platform. The model is based upon CPC (cost-per-click) and CPM's (cost per impressions), and costs are resolved by Instagram's promotion auction."The cost implication of Instagram ads are influenced by numerous factors — everything from your audience to your advertisement feedback," says Andrew Tate from AdEspresso. "A lot goes into seeing how to advertise on Instagram."AdEspresso as of late dove into $100 million worth of Instagram promotion spend in 2017, and found that the normal cost per click (CPC) for Instagram ads in Q3 ranged somewhere in the range of $0.70 and $0.80. While this is a useful benchmark it will obviously shift contingent on the sale, audience, rivalry, time of day, day of week, and so forth.

Steps to Start Advertising on Instagram

Learning the intricate details of another advertising platform may appear to be overpowering from the outset. The uplifting news here is that in case you're advertising on Facebook, there isn't a lot to learn. Actually, Instagram ads can be configured directly through Facebook Ad Manager. In case you're not advertising on Facebook, don't fuss. We'll walk you through the procedure beneath, and there is likewise the choice to make some straightforward ads legitimately inside the Instagram app. Advertisers who are further developed or running a generally huge ad set can likewise decided to configure their ads through Power Editor or Facebook's Marketing API. Instagram Partners is additionally accessible for businesses who need to purchase and deal with numerous ads, deal with an enormous network, and convey content at scale.

While configuring Instagram ads isn't excessively perplexing, there are many strides to know about. Beginning with:

1. Navigate to Facebook's Ad Manager

To navigate to ad manager inside Facebook, accepting that you're signed in to the appropriate Facebook account. Note: There is no particular Ad Manager for Instagram; Instagram ads are overseen through the Facebook Ads UI.

2. Set Your Marketing Objective

Presently for the fun part, choosing your crusade objective. Fortunately, the goals are named in a clear as crystal way. Need more traffic? Select the traffic objective. Hoping to expand brand awareness? Pick the brand awareness objective. You get the essence.

One thing to know about is that Instagram ads just work with the accompanying goals:

- Brand awareness
- App installs
- Traffic (for click throughto your website or to the app store for your app)
- Reach
- Engagement (for post engagement as it were)
- Video views
- Conversions (for conversions on your app or website)

While these objectives are natural, some join a couple of additional arrangement steps, which I'll go through here.

Brand awareness: Take an extra-long lunch. No additional means here! This is the most standard objective that will attempt to show your ads to progressively potential people prone to be interested. How does Instagram decide this? It's a mystery, yet this objective will probably uncover some new and important people to your brand.

Reach: If reach is what you're searching for (as in expanding what number of people see your ads) at that point you'll simply should make certain to choose your Instagram account while making the ad itself. It's likewise significant that in case you're hoping to run an Instagram Story ad "reach" is as of now the main target you can picked. The cool thing about this objective is that you can exploit Facebook's part trying feature, which enables you to part test two ads to see which one yields more installs.

NOTE: Split testing is additionally accessible for Traffic, App Installs, Video Views, Lead Generation, and Conversion goals.

Traffic: If you're hoping to send more people to your website or app store to download your app, this is the appropriate objective for you. The main additional means you'll have to take is choosing between those two choices, at that point enter the URL of decision, and let the traffic jam in!

Engagement: Who doesn't need more likes, offers, and by and large engagement? In the event that your objective is engagement, one thing to note is that you right now can just pay to play for "post engagement" on Instagram. Facebook will enable you to pay for "page engagement" and "occasion reactions," however this isn't at present accessible to Instagram.

App Installs: If your main goal is app installs, you've gone to the correct spot. To configure this you'll have to choose your app from the app store during set-up.

Video Views: Videos are frequently a venture of time and cash, so not advancing your video on Instagram would resemble purchasing a boarding pass to Hawaii, and leaving it in your work area. Fortunately, this goal is extremely direct, and doesn't require additional setup steps.

Lead Generation: Who doesn't need more leads? In the event that that is your main goal this objective is for you. Simply note that lead age ads don't provide the entirety of the equivalent pre-filled fields as Facebook. Instagram at present just supports email, full name, telephone number, and sexual orientation. These ads likewise have all the more an obstruction than Facebook lead age ads, since when leads click to open the ad they'll have to click through to fill out their information. On Facebook, leads can fill out their information without all the additional clicking. The other set-up piece is that you'll have to create a lead form while making your ad.

Conversions: Last, however absolutely not least, we have conversions. This goal enables you to drive your leads to make a move and convert on your website or inside your app. The additional set-up here expects you to configure either a Facebook pixel or app occasion based on the website or app you're hoping to promote; this will enable you to follow conversions.

3. Configure Your Target Audience

Since you've chosen your objective, you have to target the appropriate audience to get your ads before the correct people. This is the genuine magnificence of Instagram ads since you'll be utilizing Facebook's profundity of statistic information to reach the perfect people. On the off chance that you've done this for Facebook ads before you likely already have a few audiences assembled, and are very acquainted with the process. In case you're new to this process here's a summary of your targeting options, which you can layer to get an unequivocally targeted audience. (For instance in the event that you need to target ladies, in New York, between the ages of 19 and 65, who are interested in yoga and wellbeing nourishment, you can do only that!)

Location: Whether you need to target a nation, area, state, city, postal district, avoid or include certain spots, location targeting will enable you to do the entirety of this and then some.

Age: Allows you to target ranges from age 13 to 65+

Sex: Choose between all, men, or ladies

Dialects: Facebook suggests leaving this clear except if the language you're targeting isn't regular to the location your targeting.

Demographics: Under "Definite Targeting" you'll find demographics, which has a few sub-classifications with significantly more sub-classes under those. For instance, you can target "demographics" > "Home" > "Home Ownership" > "Leaseholders."

Interests: Interests is likewise under "Itemized Targeting" with various sub-classifications to dive into. For instance, in case you're searching for people interested in refined refreshments, sci-fi motion pictures, and flying, those options are accessible for you!

Behaviors: And one more "Point by point Targeting" choice with different sub-classifications to investigate. Regardless of whether it be buying behaviors, work jobs, commemorations, or different behaviors the options appear to be perpetual.

Associations: Here you'll have the option to target people associated with your page, app, or occasion.

Custom Audience: Custom audiences let you upload your very own rundown of contacts enabling you to target leads already in your pipeline or customers who you're looking to upsell.

Lookalike Audience: If your custom audience is tapped to their potential, create a lookalike audience. This will permit Instagram to find people who have comparative characteristics to your different audiences.

When you've configured your audience, Facebook will likewise provide you with a manual for how explicit or broad your audience.

This is a significant tool to pay attention to, in light of the fact that you need to find some kind of harmony of your audience not being excessively tremendous (since it's presumable not targeted enough), yet additionally not being excessively explicit (in the red zone), since there may not be numerous people (assuming any) to reach with such a significant number of layered targets.

App Installs: If your main goal is app installs, you've gone to the right spot. To configure this you'll need to choose your app from the app store during set-up.

Video Views: Videos are every now and again an endeavor of time and money, so not advancing your video on Instagram would take after buying a ticket to Hawaii, and leaving it in your work zone. Luckily, this goal is incredibly direct, and doesn't require additional setup steps.

Lead Generation: Who doesn't require more leads? In the event that that is your main goal this objective is for you. Just note that lead age ads don't provide the entirety of the comparable pre-filled fields as Facebook. Instagram at present just supports email, full name, phone number, and sexual direction. These ads in like manner have all the more a deterrent than Facebook lead age ads, since when leads click to open the ad they'll need to click through to fill out their information. On Facebook, leads can fill out their information without all the additional clicking. The other set-up piece is that you'll need to create a lead form while making your ad.

Conversions: Last, anyway in no way, shape or form least, we have conversions. This goal enables you to drive your leads to make a move and convert on your website or inside your app. The additional set-up here anticipates that you should configure either a Facebook pixel or app event based on the website or app you're planning to promote; this will enable you to follow conversions.

4. Configure Your Target Audience

Since you've picked your objective, you need to target the appropriate audience to get your ads before the right people. This is the authentic heavenliness of Instagram ads since you'll be using Facebook's significance of measurement information to reach the ideal people. In case you've done this for Facebook ads before you likely already have a couple of audiences amassed, and are exceptionally familiar with the process. On the off chance that you're new to this process here's a rundown of your targeting options, which you can layer to get an unequivocally targeted audience. (For instance in the event that you have to target ladies, in New York, between the ages of 19 and 65, who are interested in yoga and prosperity sustenance, you can do just that!)

Location: Whether you have to target a country, territory, state, city, postal region, maintain a strategic distance from or include certain spots, location targeting will enable you to do the entirety of this to say the very least.

Age: Allows you to target ranges from age 13 to 65+

Sex: Choose between all, men, or ladies

Vernaculars: Facebook proposes leaving this reasonable aside from if the language you're targeting isn't ordinary to the location your targeting.

Demographics: Under "Positive Targeting" you'll find demographics, which has a couple of sub-orders with fundamentally more sub-classes under those. For instance, you can target "demographics" > "Home" > "Home Ownership" > "Leaseholders."

Interests: Interests is in like manner under "Ordered Targeting" with different sub-characterizations to jump into. For instance, in the event that you're searching for people interested in refined refreshments, science fiction films, and flying, those options are open for you!

Behaviors: And one more "Point by point Targeting" decision with various sub-characterizations to research. Notwithstanding whether it be purchasing behaviors, work employments, celebrations, or various behaviors the options appear to be interminable.

Relationship: Here you'll have the choice to target people related with your page, app, or event.

Custom Audience: Custom audiences let you upload your own one of a kind overview of contacts empowering you to target leads already in your pipeline or customers who you're looking to upsell.

Lookalike Audience: If your custom audience is tapped to their potential, create a lookalike audience. This will allow Instagram to find people who have similar qualities to your various audiences.

At the point when you've configured your audience, Facebook will moreover provide you with a manual for how unequivocal or broad your audience.

This is a critical tool to pay attention to, considering the way that you have to find some sort of agreement of your audience not being too much huge (since it's apparent not targeted enough), yet additionally not being too much unequivocal (in the red zone), since there may not be various people (expecting any) to reach with such countless layered targets.

Instagram Ad Formats.

On the off chance that you are a bad decision ,aker, you might need to prepare yourself. Instagram has six ad formats to choose from. (This is path less than Facebook!) Two of those are for Instagram stories, which appear at the highest point of the feed in a way like Snapchats. The other four are formats designed for the Instagram feed, which are all the more usually utilized by advertisers.

1. Image Feed Ads

This is your most standard ad format, and likely the one you see regularly scrolling through your own feed. These ads are single images that will appear as a local encounter as your target lead is scrolling through their feed. The dazzling thing about these ads is that they don't feel like ads, particularly when done well.Here are some additional subtleties to know about:

Technical Requirements

- File type: jpg or png
- Maximum record size: 30MB

- Minimum Image Width: 600 pixels
- Image Ratio: 4:5 minimum, 16:9 most extreme
- Text length: 2,200 most extreme (*although Instagram prescribes remaining beneath 90 for ideal conveyance)
- Hashtag Number: 30 most extreme (*you can add additional in the remarks)

Supported Objectives

- Reach
- Traffic
- Conversions
- App Installs
- Lead Generation
- Brand Awareness
- Post Engagement
- Product Catalog Sales
- Store Visits

Supported Call-to-Action

- Buttons
- Apply Now
- Book Now
- Call Now
- Contact Us
- Get Directions
- Learn More
- Get Showtimes
- Download

2. Image Story Ads

Same idea as above, however these are for Instagram stories! Subtleties underneath:

Technical Requirements

- Image Ratio: 9:16 prescribed
- Minimum Image Width: 600 pixels

Supported Objectives

- Reach
- Traffic

- Conversions
- App Installs
- Lead Generation

Supported Call-to-Action

- Buttons
- Apply Now
- Book Now
- Contact Us
- Download

3. Video Feed Ads

Breath life into your ad with a video! If you've placed the time in to make a quality video, at that point you ought to totally be advancing it through your Instagram feed. While most video records are supported by Instagram, they prescribe utilizing H.264 pressure, square pixels, fixed edge rate, dynamic output, and stereo AAC sound pressure at 128kbps+ (PRO TIP: if your video isn't meeting these prerequisite you can generally run it through the video transcoder, Handbrake, to make these adjustments).

Technical Requirements

- Video Resolution: 1080 x 1080 pixels (at any rate)
- Maximum file size: 4GB
- Video Ratio: 4:5 minimum, 16:9 maximum
- Video Duration: 60 seconds maximum
- Video Captions: discretionary
- Image Ratio: 4:5 minimum, 16:9 maximum
- Text length: 125 characters maximum suggested
- Hashtag Number: 30 maximum (*you can add additional in the remarks)

Supported Objectives

- Reach
- Traffic
- Conversions
- Lead Generation
- Brand Awareness
- Post Engagement
- Store Visits

Supported Call-to-Action

- Buttons
- Apply Now
- Book Now
- Call Now
- Contact Us
- Download

4. Video Story Ads

This is another great spot to run video ads, since stories are the place clients regularly hope to see videos, so the "selling" part of advertising doesn't feel as constrained. The suggested video specs for uploading are equivalent to recorded above, and here are some additional subtleties to remember!

Technical Requirements

- Video Resolution: 1080 x 1920 pixels (in any event)
- Maximum file size: 4GB
- Video Ratio: 9:16 maximum
- Video Duration: 15 seconds maximum
- Video Captions: not accessible

Supported Objectives

- Reach
- Traffic
- Conversions
- Lead Generation
- App Installs

Supported Call-to-Action

- Buttons
- Apply Now
- Book Now
- Call Now
- Contact Us
- Download

5. Carousel Feed Ads

Next we have carousel feed ads. How fun are these! This format enables you to show a progression of scrollable images as opposed to only one single image. This ad type great for extremely visual brands, similar to those in the nourishment business, furniture sellers, clothing options, get-away destinations, vehicle vendors, and so on. Yet, they're not just for "hot" businesses; they can likewise work to refine your brand or show off your way of life by showing the people behind your product or money related company. The carousel format enables you to choose from up to 10 images inside a solitary ad, each with its own link. Video is likewise a possibility for these ads.

Technical Requirements

- File type: jpg or png
- Maximum file size: 30MB
- Minimum Image Width: 600 pixels
- Image Ratio: 4:5 minimum, 16:9 maximum
- Text length: 2,200 maximum (*although Instagram recommends staying below 90 for optimal delivery)
- Video Duration: 60 seconds maximum
- Hashtag Number: 30 maximum (*you can add additional in the comments)

Supported Objectives

- Reach
- Traffic
- Conversions
- Brand Awareness
- Lead Generation
- Product Catalog Sales

Supported Call-to-Action

- Buttons
- Apply Now
- Book Now
- Contact Us
- Call Now
- Download

6. Canvas Story Ads

And last, but definitely not least, we have the newest addition to the ad format family, Canvas ads. There ads are truly immersive, allowing advertising to create a 360 VR experience within their story. They're only supported via mobile devices, and extremely customizable for the advertiser, but you will need some technical chops. These ads work with image, video, and carousel. Check out this guide to learn more about Canvas ads.

Technical Requirements

- Minimum Image Width: 400 pixels
- Minimum Image Height: 150 pixels

Supported Objectives

- Reach
- Brand Awareness

- Traffic
- Conversions
- Lead Generation
- Post Engagement
- Video Views
- Store Visits

Supported Call-to-Action

- Buttons
- Apply Now
- Book Now
- Contact Us

5 INSTAGRAM ADVERTISING BEST PRACTICES

Since you have the fundamental standards of Instagram advertising down, the time has come to get the most elevated ROI conceivable by following these prescribed procedures to create great Instagram ads.

1. Instill Each Ad with Personality

Regardless of whether it be an amusing goof, a passionate video, or only a captivating image showing off your way of life, on the off chance that your Instagram post doesn't feel acculturated, at that point you won't reach your engagement potential. People use

Instagram to be engaged, diverted, or flabbergasted. Regardless of whether it's while you're on the train to work or when you are loosening up in the wake of a monotonous day of work, nobody is hoping to bounce on Instagram to see an exhausting corporate advertisement. This is the reason appealing to feelings is consistently the best approach. Look at this fun post from Shape Magazine as an ideal model.

2. Make Sure Your Ad Is Contextually Relevant

What works with one social media platform won't really work with another. For instance, your business likely wouldn't promote a similar content through LinkedIn as they would through Twitter, as the audience is typically in an alternate perspective. The equivalent goes for Instagram. Put yourself in your target purchaser's shoes and know about where they are. On Instagram, do you think your lead is probably going to download and read your 40 page digital book? Most likely not. Guarantee your ads don't feel excessively sales-driven in light of the fact that this isn't typically what Instagram is utilized for.

3. Use Hashtags…

Be that as it may, don't simply hashtag #food or #love. Get progressively inventive, and do some client research to see which hashtags are bound to be searched for by your audience. Likewise, don't try too hard with hashtags. This can make your post look somewhat messy and desperate. The ideal number? TrackMaven broke down 65,000 posts and found that 9 hashtags is the ideal number for most elevated post engagement. They likewise found that longer hashtags regularly perform better.

4. Run a Contest

Advancing a contest or giveaway is by a wide margin one of the best approaches to reach your goals quicker with Instagram advertising. Why? Since people love competition and free stuff! What better approach to get your audience amped up for your brand?

5. Post at Optimal Hours

If you realize your audience well, this shouldn't be too difficult to even consider determining, yet experimentation can likewise work here. Consider your vertical. In case you're an online retailer, when do people commonly search for clothing on the web? Or then again in case you're a vehicle vendor, what days of the week do you see the most noteworthy spike in website traffic? Posing these inquiries is a decent spot to begin. Right away, put forward and advertise on Instagram! This is one platform you ought not disregard, and this guide ought to give you enough assets to become insta-famous.

Monitoring and moderating

What are these stats?

• The number of clicks: this refers to the number of clicks your Ad has received from users

• The Post likes: this refers to the number of likes your Ad has achieved

• The Cost per click: this refers to the total cost of each click on your Ad

• The Cost per view: this refers to the total cost per impression of your Ad

• Click through rates: this refers to the percentage of clicks through to your landing page the Ad has achieved in relation to the number of impressions

• Cost per lead: this refers to the overall cost of gaining a lead via your Ad

• Lead to customer conversion: this refers to the number of leads who become your customers via your Instagram Ad

The number of clicks and post likes you receive on your Ad will give you an idea of the efficiency of the image you have chosen: the more clicks, the better the image.

The cost per click (CPC), the cost per view and the cost per lead are the figures that represent how much the advertising process is costing you at each step: the most important figure being the cost per lead, as this tells you exactly how much each new lead acquired via your campaign has cost your company. Another important figure is the lead to customer conversion, which is the number of leads who go on to become customers as a direct result of this Ad.

The click through rate (CTR) is also an important figure, as it will tell you the percentage of users who not only saw your Ad, but who actually followed your call to action straight through to your website or landing page. This number will give you an idea of how effective your image and text choices for your Ad are at getting attention and deserving clicks.

INFLUENCER MARKETING RESEARCH TOOLS

If you decided not to use a platform or an agency for your influencer marketing then you will have to build up relationships with influencers yourself. To do this, you first need to know the influencers that rule your niche. If you are an active online participant in your niche you may already possess a good idea who are the best influencers. In other cases, you will have to carry out considerable research first. Luckily there are a variety of influencer marketing tools to help you in your quest.

In the event that you are searching for an agency to run your campaign - feel free to utilize our agency coordinating structure underneath and you will be coordinated with the most appropriate agency for your needs. You should think about where you would like to find your potential influencers. Many operate via web-based networking media, so a portion of these tools center around finding the notable people in the internet based life channels. You should initially think about where your intended interest group invests its energy. If you target more seasoned people, for instance, you will frequently search for influencers in Facebook groups discussing your niche. In the event that your objective market is youngsters, at that point you may concentrate more on Snapchat, Youtube or Instagram. Numerous influencers have picked up their popularity from blogs they compose. We have a couple of tools here that assist you with finding the persuasive bloggers in your niche.

There is a lot of proof that influencer marketing can be an exceptionally effective strategy for spreading a brand's message. At the point when the Influencer Marketing Hub attempted an overview on the condition of influencer marketing a year ago, we found that the normal earned media esteem per $1 spent on influencer marketing was a profoundly respectable $7.65.We have likewise observed a fast ascent in the utilization of Instagram in the course of the most recent couple of years, to the point where it would now be able to guarantee more than 800 million month to month dynamic clients. Instagram Stories has likewise observed quick growth and is currently has a greater number of clients than Snapchat.

It makes sense for most brands to work with influencers on Instagram. In any case, on the off chance that you will do that you need first to find influencers who are happy to work with you. On the off chance that you depend on building connections naturally, suitable influencers can be trying to find, and it will be a time-devouring procedure to create and support connections. That is the place the influencer platforms can give a helpful assistance. Influencer platforms can be a definitive tool to disentangle your influencer marketing. Various platforms have practical experience in the services they offer, however the most well-known ones are:

- Influencer discovery
- Relationship management
- Campaign management
- Influencer marketplace
- Third party analytics
- Influencer content amplification

Every one of the platforms centers around giving influencer services to particular interpersonal organizations. With Instagram quickly turning into the network of decision for influencers, it is nothing unexpected that by far most of influencer platforms include Instagram in their contributions. Here are the leading influencer platforms for Instagram that can assist you with your influencer search and make your influencer marketing a smoother, progressively streamlined procedure.

1. AspireIQ (formerly known as Revfluence)

AspireIQ (some time ago Revfluence) has the profiles of more than 500,000 influencers in its discovery motor. Its calculation creeps the web searching through social accounts to find people who meet its influencer criteria. In any case, if an influencer needs to effectively participate in campaigns through the AspireIQ platform, they first need to pick into the framework. AspireIQ gives various approaches to brands to find influencers. You can search utilizing applicable watchwords, points, or hashtags, and afterward filter accounts by whatever strategy you need. You can utilize the "Quickmatch" feature, which recommends influencers based on your inclinations. Another way you can find influencers is to utilize AspireIQ's Watchlist feature, which will disclose to you which influencers have referenced you or your rivals. You can even search by picture – searching for influencers who have shared content like a particular picture. AspireIQ covers significantly more than just influencer discovery, be that as it may. It has powerful tools that can help brands with:

- Campaign creation

- Campaign lifecycle management

- Digital term sheets

- Product following

- Content cooperation

- Trackable sales links

- Creator execution spreadsheet

- Campaign analytics

- Payments

2. Neoreach

Neoreach has manufactured a calculation that digs the social web for information. Their database contains the social subtleties of more than 3 million influencers. The company targets huge organizations and undertakings.

You start your influencer search with keywords, and afterward refine the outcomes utilizing a range of factors, including:

- Conversation point
- Social channel
- Social measurements
- Audience psychographics and demographics.

It gives you an abundance of data, and you can sort influencers into groups or campaigns. Neoreach additionally utilizes AI to prescribe suitable influencers for your needs. The more you use Neoreach, the more accurate their proposals will be. When you have discovered influencers, you can utilize Neoreach's campaign management tools to help your influencer marketing run all the more easily. It includes an incorporated interchanges center point, to keep the whole influencer relationship process together. Campaign reports are exceptionally nitty gritty, letting you know for all intents and purposes anything there is to think about campaign execution. Neoreach has built up their own proportion of ROI – Influencer Media Value (IMV). You just need to connect your advertising spend to the model, and Neoreach will give you an accurate gauge of IMV for your future influencer campaigns.

Services Offered: Influencer Discovery, Campaign Management

3. Upfluence

Upfluence has made significant changes to its offerings over the last year. It has narrowed the range of services it offers, concentrating on what it believes are its strengths. The heart of Upfluence is its massive database containing nearly 1 million influencers. It indexes and updates social profiles in real time, analyzing every item of content for reach and engagement. Brands can search Upfluence to find influencers using any combination of relevant keywords. They can then drill down and refine their selection of influencers. You can even weight your keywords, placing more emphasis on some than others. You can filter by audience data, including psychographic attributes like cultural interests and brand affinities. Upfluence allows you to make lists of potential influencers meeting various criteria, which you can export into CSV files. You can manage your influencer within Upfluence, including keeping a central repository for all email correspondence. The lifecycle management function keeps track of your progress with each influencer.

Services Offered: Influencer Discovery, Campaign Management

4. Tagger Media

Tagger Media is a pick in influencer marketplace with more than 1 million influencers in its database. It tracks 8 billion social discussions that make more than 28 million information focuses. You can search for influencers utilizing 50 filters to assist you with refining the outcomes. Tagger Media offers substantially more than only an influencer search motor, be that as it may. It is a full influencer marketplace, designed to enable huge businesses to find and work with its monstrous database of influencers.It is an across the board platform that enables brands to:

- Perform point by point searches on the database of clients

- Discover influencers to work with

- Create campaigns, making them just accessible to welcomed influencers or then again to anyone

- Manage chose influencers and their content entries

- Analyze post and influencer execution
- Determine important ROI

Tagger Media puts a critical accentuation on psychographics. It investigations what people are discussing, their inclinations and their affinities. This enables clients to comprehend what content will drive engagement. It likewise features an exceptionally vigorous management dashboard, making it easy for firms to arrange their influencer marketing endeavors.

Services Offered: Influencer Discovery, Campaign Management, Influencer Marketplace, Third Party Analytics.

5. Julius

Julius has grown from being exclusively an influencer discovery motor into a fully-fledged self-administration marketing suite. Despite everything it features an incredible influencer search motor, in any case, with a variety of information identifying with its 120,000 fully checked influencers. You can search for influencers utilizing 50 unique criteria to limit your search. These spread both statistic and psychographic factors. Julius enables you to add any influencers you presently work with who aren't already in their framework. The Julius staff vet these people and add their applicable information to the database. Julius gives you various approaches to search for suitable influencers. It features a particularly easy-to-utilize interface. You can search by criteria identifying with potential influencers, your intended interest group, or social reach and engagement. You can rapidly make records based on the criteria you are utilizing. Julius likewise features a strong arrangement of campaign management tools, again designed In a reasonable, easy-to-utilize style. You can without much of a stretch find out anything you need to think about your campaign with only a couple of catch clicks. The strong clean approach extends to announcing too. It gives clear easy-to-read perceptions of your influencers' presentation on each campaign.

Services Offered: Influencer Discovery, Campaign Management, Third Party Analytics.

6. HYPR

HYPR has built a massive database of more than 10 million influencers and makes a point of collecting as much demographic data about their followers as possible. They consider their search engine to be "talent agnostic," i.e., they don't limit their results to showing just a list of influencers who have agreed to work with them. The search engine is the heart of HYPR. It is very much the Google of influencers. It uses a simple, but highly responsive interface, leading to a quick return of search results. Although you could search for an influencer you know by name, the bulk of your searches will be by audience. HYPR believes the key to successful influencer marketing is matching up influencer with target audiences. You can search by audience interest and by a range of demographic factors, such as gender, ethnicity, and age group. You can then refine your searches further, by looking at factors such as influencer location and follower counts. Once you have made your list, HYPR will present you with influencers who meet your criteria. Each influencer shows up on a little card, showing their photo and a summary of relevant details. If you believe somebody looks suitable, you can click on their card to see more information about their audience and social reach.

Services Offered: Influencer Discovery

7. MAVRCK

As its name indicates, Mavrck aims to take a different approach to influencer marketing. Most platforms will provide you with a list of people who are already popular on social media but don't necessarily know your product. Mavrck's approach is to take your existing customers and encourage them to promote your product online. Mavrck takes your existing customer list and determines who has the most influence online. You begin by setting up a white-labeled standalone website, or you add a plugin to your existing website. Customers log into your site using their Facebook profile. Mavrck finds all the public social data connected to each customer. It can then use its algorithm to determine each customer's social influence.

If Mavrck finds a customer to be sufficiently influential it automatically activates a suitable campaign for him or her. Mavrck has a list of 20 'digital activities' different customer influencers can do, depending on their level of influence. Your customers receive rewards for completing each 'digital activity' you offer them. You can use all of the content created by your micro-influencer customers to attract new customers – who may, in turn, become micro-influencers on behalf of your brand. Mavrck provides you with a detailed dashboard showing a considerable amount of information about your campaigns.

Services Offered: Influencer Discovery, Relationship Management, Campaign Management, Influencer Marketplace, Third Party Analytics.

8. Influencer

Influencer tags itself as being "run by creators, for creators." Indeed its Chief Marketing Officer (CMO) is Caspar Lee, who is renowned as a YouTube star. It's founder, Ben Jeffries, was only 18 when he started the business. It is very much a product of Generation Z. With Influencer being run by influencers, it should be easy to distinguish genuine influencers. It is fussier about who it accepts onto their books. They are only interested in people with many real followers and a high level of engagement. This means that Influencer has established a reputation as only working with talent who can easily communicate with their followers. This means that customers will only find about 1,000 influencers on their database – but they are all highly influential onliners. Because Influencer has a more hands-on process than their more automated competitors, it does limit itself geographically. It is headquartered in the UK and currently focuses on influencers who have audiences based in Europe. Although Influencer is a platform, it offers many of the features of a boutique agency. It includes all the expected management tools to assist with your campaigns.

Services Offered: Influencer Marketplace.

9. Traackr

Traackr is one of the earliest influencer marketing tools – the first Traackr product was released in 2008. The company has changed its offerings as the industry developed and now specializes in influencer relationship management, built on top of an impressive online platform with an array of influencer management tools. Although the platform focuses more on influencer relationship than influencer discovery, it does include a robust search engine. It provides numerous search and filter options to help brands find the ideal influencers for their campaigns. Traackr takes a hybrid approach to its influencer database – a combination of human involved in curation mixed with algorithms collecting data. Traackr offers you many ways you can organize your selected influencers. One of these is to sort your influencers by relationship stage. This makes it easy to segment your influencers by how close you are. Traackr allows you to customize the data you store about your influencers. It also records all communications you or members of your team have with them. Traackr incorporates a social listening tool which allows you to track your influencer content in real time. You can filter this however you want, so you are not swamped by irrelevant details. Another useful tool is Traackr's network visualization map. This shows you how influencers are connected with other people, both within and outside your network. This gives you a clear idea of who influences your influencers, and may give you further suggestions for building relationships. Traackr provides a powerful set of campaign management tools, that makes running campaigns appear simple. You can even track how much your campaigns influence conversation.

Services Offered: Relationship Management, Campaign Management

DECIDING YOUR PRICE AS AN INFLUENCER

Instagram influencer rates are one of online networking's best-kept secrets. Sure, there are murmurs and bits of gossip, similar to Kendall Jenner's accounted for $250,000 pull for her Fyre Festival underwriting on Instagram. In any case, what precisely are the computations that go into making influencer marketing a $6.5 billion industry？For a plethora of Instagram influencers, a sponsored post includes a lot more work than posting an orange square. (For those not aware of everything, Fyre Festival promoters made buzz by paying large scale influencers to post an orange jpeg.)Creating branded content includes time, work, ability, and creation costs. What's more, those things aren't paid for with products and freebies.And paying the correct value pays off. In any case, what is the privilege price? Read on to find the best recipe for figuring rates, the advantages of various sponsorship plans, and different elements that may influence influencer valuing.

The fundamental equation for figuring reasonable Instagram influencer rates

There are numerous elements that decide the rate an influencer charges for their work. Most estimating beginnings with this gauge recipe and goes up from that point. $100 x 10,000 followers + additional items = all out rate Typically, influencers will have a press pack portraying their rates and the sorts of partnerships accessible. Contingent upon the crusade, bundled content or exceptional rates can likewise be worked out to lessen work and costs.

What kind of influencer is directly for your objectives?

From individual fund to plant-based influencers, there are micro, full scale, and power center influencers in each class. Contingent upon your Instagram marketing objectives, certain influencers might be a superior counterpart for your brand.

If your objective is brand-awaareness

For brands hoping to make far reaching buzz, full scale influencers with enormous supporter accounts might be the best wagered. Full scale influencers ordinarily have in excess of 200,000 followers, which gives them the capacity to reach a more extensive group of spectators.

If your objective is conversions

An influencer's engagement rate is one of the most dependable approaches to foresee changes on Instagram. Engagement rates can be determined by including up all engagements a post (likes, remarks, clicks, shares), isolating by adherent tally, and increasing by 100. The normal engagement rate on Instagram is 2.1 percent.

If your objective is changes, an influencer's engagement rate may matter more than supporter check. Here's the place control center influencers (25,000-200,000 followers) regularly come in. For instance, a power-center influencer with 179K followers and a high engagement rate will probably be a superior partner than a full scale influencer with a lower engagement rate. Some influencers may charge more than $100 per 10,000 followers in the event that they have a higher than normal rate of engagement.

If your goal is to gain a niche audience

Micro influencers have 25,000 followers or less, and are all the time mainstream in area or subject explicit networks. They work in a range of businesses of classes, including anything from sports and gaming, to travel and nourishment. Group of spectators sizes of niche influencers can range from micro to full scale. For instance, excellence influencer Hudda Kattan has an astounding 33 million followers. In the event that your brand falls into a niche classification, it's advantageous to delineate the micro influencers in your industry's social network. A decent brand fit is imperative to influencers, and will prompt an increasingly authentic and effective battle. Niche influencers may charge more than the essential rate for the mastery they bring to their particular group of spectators.

Types of Instagram posts and partnerships

There are various approaches to collaborate with influencers on Instagram. Here we separate the principle things and arrangements Instagram influencers charge for. We additionally feature every one of their unique benefits.

Instagram photo

A standard sponsored Instagram post ordinarily includes a photo and caption. Sometimes the product is included in the picture. In different cases, similar to when an assistance is being promoted, the caption is increasingly significant.

Benefits of an Instagram photo:

- It's anything but difficult to foresee and follow post execution.

- Partnership disclaimers can be added obviously. Product and brand labeling can be added.

- Tagging can be fortified in the caption too.

- Super short links can be added to the caption.

- Allows for authentic narrating.

- Can be additionally promoted in an Instagram story.

Instagram slideshow

The key distinction between an Instagram post and slideshow is that a slideshow permits an influencer to build to a greater degree a story, or showcase the sponsorship in various ways. Nonetheless, added content will include added costs–particularly if various shoots are required.

Benefits of an Instagram slideshow:

- Offers numerous ways for a group of people to connect with content.

- Features various products or use-cases for your brand.

- Creates more space for an influencer to include their authentic take.

- Allows for increasingly unpredictable or nuanced narrating.

Instagram video

Video's star continues to rise on social, and Instagram is no different, tracking an 80 % year-over-year increment. Most content creators appreciate that a video involves greater production costs than a photo, but the added investment can often translate into more than just added engagement.

Benefits of Instagram video:

- Gives the influencer a voice, literally.
- This often shows the influencer's audience a new side person they follow.
- Allows for compelling storytelling.
- Builds bundling potential. Consider working teasers or behind-the-scenes posts or Instagram Stories into a video shoot.

Instagram giveaway or contest

Instagram contests are a great method to grow brand awareness and followers. Commonly a contest involves approaching a client to accomplish something for a chance to win a prize, regardless of whether it's labeling a friend, preferring your account, or sharing a post.

Benefits of an Instagram contest:

•	Reaches a wider extensive group of spectators with a little cost-per-engagemcnt.

•	Earns group of audience data, particularly if your contest involves a brief like "remark with your fantasy destination and label a friend."

•	Puts your product or administration up front.

Instagram Story

An Instagram story is basically a photo or video that evaporates following 24 hours. Production quality can range from without any preparation cell phone film to cleaned uploaded content, and costs will differ in like manner

Benefits of an Instagram Story

Regularly looks increasingly easygoing and authentic.

Permits the influencer to include character through GIFs, markups, and sticks.

Noticeable labeling can be added all the more effectively.

Influencers can be valuable about their feed's stylish, yet will in general be progressively adaptable with Story content.

One disadvantage about Instagram Stories is that they're more enthusiastically to follow.

Instagram's API offers restricted retrievable information. That and they vanish except if featured (you can pay extra to have your content included in an influencers Story Highlights).

Instagram Story with swipe up

The swipe up feature on Instagram is a consistent method to acquire in-application conversions. Also, since links are difficult to find in Instagram's environment, story swipe ups have added esteem. Contingent upon the influencer, swipe ups can cost more.

Benefits of an Instagram Story with swipe up:

•	Provides a cost-viable approach to acquire changes and quality leads.

•	Allows your brand to include setting with a particular or custom greeting page.

•	Offers a dependable way to check group of spectators enthusiasm for your brand.

- Brings customers a bit nearer to making a buy.

In case you're working with a micro-influencer that has less than 10,000 followers or isn't confirmed, they might not approach this feature.

Instagram Story with poll

Adding a poll to an Instagram Story is a low-cost way to learn more about an influencer's followers (and your prospective customers).

Benefits of an Instagram Story with a poll:

Captures immediate feedback from the influencer's audience in a fun way.

Posting poll results is another low-cost way to increase exposure by another 24 hours.

Brand takeover

A brand takeover usually involves hosting the influencer's content on your brand's feed for an agreed upon length of time. A takeover agreement may involve asks for the influencer to promote it a certain number of times from their account–in posts and/or Stories.

Benefits of a brand takeover:

- Brings the influencer's followers to your account.
- Helps to increase brand awareness.

- Promotes influencer's content and perspective, which often comes across as more authentic.
- Opens the door for bundle or special rate agreements. Influencers should always be paid, but if your brand can offer special tours or access, that can be factored in as well.

Story Highlights

Having an influencer highlight branded stories extends the expiry date of that content. This will also put your brand in prime real estate on their account's profile. However, high visibility like this will come at a higher cost.

Benefits of Story Highlights

- Maximum exposure. On an Instagram profile, highlights are positioned above the feed, meaning brand placement here is a step above photos or videos.
- Stories won't be highlighted forever, but they live longer than 24 hours and increase the odds that they'll reach more viewers.
- Increases conversions. If the highlighted story includes a swipe-up, it's likely you'll earn more visits and leads, for a longer time.

Link in Bio

The only place where links are active on Instagram is in a person's account bio. If you're planning to sponsor an influencer post, it may be worthwhile to invest more by asking them to promote a link from their bio.

Benefits of Link in Bio:

- Prime visibility. Someone may miss a post or story, but if they visit an influencer's profile they'll see your link. Consider asking the influencer to include a call-to-action in their bio as well.
- Increases traffic. If your brand is angling to drive visitors to a certain webpage, this is one of the best ways to do it on

Instagram.IGTV

IGTV is the longer form video vertical on Instagram. It has pride of place on the platform, appearing at the top of the feed, in the explore tab, and next to highlights on a user's feed. Because IGTV typically involves higher production and has high visibility, it will involve higher costs.

Benefits of IGTV:

- Boosts visibility of content in the app.
- If the influencer is verified and has enough followers, they can post vertical videos up to 60

- minutes in length, allowing for long-form storytelling.
- IGTV videos can include clickable links.

Other factors that affect Instagram influencer pricing

Brands in search of quality partnerships should budget for these cost factors when marketing with influencers.

Usage rights

If you want to maintain ownership of the content you create with an influencer, so that you can use it on other platforms or down the line, this will likely impact the influencer's rate.

Production fees

Various production related costs such as how long it takes to produce the content (labor), props, clothing, hair and makeup, photography, editing, and travel, should be factored into influencer rates.

Agency fees

Many influencers are represented by managers or agencies such as Crowdtap, Niche, Tapinfluencer, or Maker Studios. These companies will typically charge handling fees.

Campaign length

The length of the campaign will have a direct affect on influencer pricing based on the added labour, content, and exclusivity requirements attached to it.

Timing

Depending on how much time a brand gives an influencer to create content, a rush fee may be applied.

Exclusivity

Most contracts include an exclusivity clause, in which the influencer agrees not to work with competitors for a determined length of time. Since this could cost influencers prospective deals, it will affect the cost.

Brand fit

If an influencer feels that a company lacks a level of affinity with their personal brand, they may charge for what the partnership may cost them in credibility.

Experts in the field of marketing likewise discovered that, the best method to reach out to potential buyers in this century would be through the people these buyers pursue and trust on social stages like Instagram. It's basic extremely: A lot of people trust the proposals of genuine people, other than those of sponsors. As time cruises by, innovation has made more ways for people to debilitate and square promotions. Further constraining organizations to reach out to influencers to get their products and brand before their potential buyers. Be that as it may, the issue a lot of influencers have is realizing the amount they should charge their clients. Many do not have the required data and frantically need to know whether they are under or cheating their clients.

At the point when you get enlisted to do a sponsored post, it's not quite the same as customary content creation, on the grounds that the brand is paying for you to post – which implies: introduction, eyeballs, sees, clicks (you get where we're going with this). This is the reason you should consistently be straightforward with your examination and your influence.

If you don't feel like your capacity to drive clicks is there at this time, be forthright with the brand and tell them that you might want to create a specific measure of photos for them notwithstanding posting on Instagram. Along these lines you can post a couple on your page, yet in addition send them extra photos for them to post on their account on the grounds that toward the day's end, each brand is consistently needing great Instagram photos for their feed as well. Furthermore, when you are not certain about the intensity of your influence, the key is to OVERDELIVER.

Asking the brand for a budget.

You ought to consistently begin any sponsorship discussion with asking what their budget is (obviously you ought to have a main concern as a primary concern since anything lower than that number is simply not justified, despite any potential benefits to you).By approaching the brand for their budget first, you can (a) think of a proposition dependent on their needs, (b) save yourself time from making a recommendation that isn't in their value run and the in particular (c) save yourself from passing up additional cold hard cash… imagine a scenario where they are eager to pay WAY more than what you were anticipating proposing. In any case, imagine a scenario where they state there is no budget and they need you to do the post for exchange. Sadly, free swag doesn't pay the bills – yet a little doesn't hurt, correct? Obviously there are consistently special cases if it's an item or experience you need in your life! We've worked with celebrity influencers (2+ million followers) who have gone on trips for nothing due to every one of the advantages that join them.

So at last, every partnership or sponsorship descends how might this benefit YOU! What's more, in case you're consulting with a travel industry board or lodging that has offered to pay for the entirety of your movement costs, and you have another brand ready to pay for a sponsorship, at that point you'll need to tell them that you'll be bringing along a sponsor to pay for ability expenses. To make sure you know, 9 times out of 10, the travel industry loads up will cover flights, housing, transport, nourishment, drink and exercises, yet perhaps nothing else outside of that. That is the reason you'll need to reach out to another brand (that lines up with the destination), to check whether they are keen on having their products shot in the fascinating destination, to assist you with getting paid.

Be that as it may, remember to be proficient and make sure the sponsor willing to pony up money lines up with the destination you are made a beeline for in light of the fact that else it might cause issues. For instance, asking a caffeinated drink company to sponsor an outing to Costa Rica, would not make sense with Costa Rica's homestead to table ethos. We're enthusiastic about press trip manners since we know how significant cultivating connections are and how these trips can really find you more occupations not far off. Finally, we must pressure this as much as possible – don't simply accept the position due to the cash. Continuously make sure every partnership and sponsorship you acknowledge lines up with your brand esteems and objectives… essentially, don't be shallow.

Instagram Price per Post – The Basics

Before we delve into the nitty gritty on pricing, we need to define "post" because it will determine how you price yourself.

- Instagram post – photo: posting a permanent post on your Instagram account using specific hashtags, tags, geotags etc.
- Instagram post – video: posting a permanent video on your Instagram account using specific hashtags, tags, geotags and even an audio mention.
- Instagram story: promoting on a story and using a specific hashtag and tag and even an audio mention.

And if you work in an Instagram story, you'll have the option to provide it on your Instagram "highlights" as an additional value added feature. According to Adweek, the average price per sponsored post is about $300, with influencers that have 100,000 followers earning closer to $800 a post. While everyone wants a magic formula, we know there is no one-size-fits-all approach…this is the wild west, after all! That's why we're covering three different ways you can establish your "insta rate." So for all those wondering "how much is my instagram post worth," below are three different ways to come up with your price.

OPTION 1: Charge An Hourly Rate

Charging by an hourly rate can be a great option for beginners who don't have a large following or engagement but still feel like you could produce quality content. This is a good bet for micro-influencers (less than 10,000 organic, authentic followers).Opting for an hourly rate is also great for a freelancer with a special skillset (i.e. graphic design, copywriter, photographer etc). You can also offer different hourly rates depending on what exactly you will be doing for the brand. In some cases, people like to charge more for their time if it involves a technical skill. For example, if you're reviewing a product versus creating a video or taking product photos- the latter two involve way more effort which means you should be compensated for your time. If you're using a drone, doing any special effects or using some technical editing skills, you may want to charge more for that time as well.

So what's the formula?

- Hourly rate (* hours needed to produce) + any extra costs
- Optional: Hourly rate (* hours needed to produce) + Speciality Hourly Rate (* hours needed to produce) + any extra costs

Any additional expenses could include the accompanying – props, colleague work, travel costs and so on. Everyones hourly rate is distinctive dependent on what they have to make a living so you have to apparition what works for you. Also, with regards to really charging for your hours, make sure to keep it sorted out and record the entirety of your time, including thought age, the time it takes you to really make the content (photograph or video), altering time and so forth. Note that there's likewise the typical expense of working together. For instance, if you drive to a plan store to purchase props for your shoot, would you say you are going to charge for that time or for the gas you spent to arrive? This is up to you and your association with the brand. You can bundle it into your fee or give it to them as a kindness credit (and show them on your invoice that you didn't charge for x, y, z).

A few people pass by the way of thinking that time is cash and you have to charge for consistently. Others are more careless on this and simply bundle in basic assignments since they don't have any desire to be viewed as "nickel and diming." It's truly up to you and what you feel great doing – after all it is your business! One thing to consistently remember is that a few brands dislike paying you constantly so you should gauge the all out time it will take you and afterward quote them a flat fee. Indeed, it might wind up requiring some investment than you foreseen, or you may complete somewhat sooner than anticipated however why a company may lean toward a flat fee over an hourly charge is they know precisely what's in store and can budget for the expense.

In case you're charging for costs, make sure to just include direct expenses related with each assignment. On the off chance that you did an expert shoot and purchased everybody in your group a Starbucks latte, that was your decision and NOT something we would encourage you to include on your invoice. Here is a model for doing a sponsored post for a sunglass company and you've set your hourly rate at $50:

Sponsored Post Creation: $50/hour

Hours Spent/Or Hours Estimated: 3.5

- 30 minutes researching brand + their rivals
- 1 hour choosing innovative course of photos + all styling
- 45 minutes to shoot item
- 1 hour experiencing photos and altering chooses
- 15 minutes to post and draft inscription

Total: $175

In this case, for micro-influencers, we would suggest providing the brand with the high resolution images you post as well as a few "courtesy photos." So if you provide them with 4 photos total (including the photo you posted), this means the brand paid around $43 per photo (your rate of $175/4 photos). You should then give them the option to purchase additional photos from your roll. If you shot the photos anyway, you might as well try to make some extra cash from them!

OPTION 2: Charge By Using Your Average Engagements Per Post

Some people don't feel comfortable charging an hourly rate. This could be for different reasons but the most common one is that many creatives find it difficult to keep track of every minute they spend on a project. That's why you may want to consider solely charging for your influence and posting on social.

Logically, it makes sense to charge per engagement because on top of an image or video you produce, that is really what the brand is getting in return. It is important to understand that there is an inverse relationship between engagement and follower growth. This means that the more your followers and fans grow, the lower your engagement tends to be. This could be because once you're receiving 30,000+ likes a photo, your audience may not want to give you that "extra like" because they don't think you need it. We know that sounds strange but hey, we don't make the rules. So in terms of pricing yourself for engagement, let's say you receive an average of 3,000 likes a photo and

75 comments per post. The way you can find your average likes is sum up the likes of the last 12 photos you've posted and divide by 12. This math is the same for comments.

Average likes: Total # of likes for last 12 posts / 12

Average comments: Total # of comments for the last 12 posts / 12

Then you would sum up the average likes + average comments to get your average engagement per post.

Average engagement per post = average likes + average comments

You then can establish your fee per engagement (i.e. what is your like, story view or comment worth). Since comments show a higher level of engagement, you can charge a brand more for every REAL COMMENT than a like. Because we like to keep it real, if you are in a comment pod or do any shady business – do yourself a favor and do NOT charge for non-organic comments. This is not an authentic engagement and therefore you shouldn't charge for it. Since you've already spent the time shooting the photo to post, you may as well charge less for a sponsored post and have them purchase additional posts. For example, rather than doing just one post, how about offering them 3 posts with a 30% discount. It's a win-win for everyone because you have to do the upfront work anyway to post just one photo, and they're getting the most bang for their buck with the discount you offered them.

And if you're curious about Insta Story rates, you can charge based on the number of average views you get per story, using the same rate you charge per like and based on the same formula. Remember, brands like to feel like they are receiving more than they bargained for (just like you do) so creating packages with discounts is always a win!

OPTION 3: Charge By Using Your CPM Rate

If we need to delve deeper in the marketing scene, we'll fill you in on a typical term – CPM. CPM is the cost for each 1,000 impressions of an advertisement. In any case, why the "M" in CPM? It really represents the Roman Numeral for 1,000. So how would you figure out your CPM Rate? Only 3 simple advances and you're good to go!

Stage 1: You'll need to initially figure out your engagement rate:

(Normal preferences + Average remarks per post/absolute # of followers) * 100

When you have your engagement rate you can utilize the table beneath to perceive the amount you can charge per thousand of followers.

CPM Value Table:

- 1.5-3% engagement = $5 CPM

- 3-5% engagement = $7 CPM

- 5-8% engagement = $10 CPM

- 8% engagement = $15 CPM

Stage 2: Next, you'll have to take the absolute # of followers you have and separate it by 1000.

- If you have 1000 followers, that # will be 10

- If you have 50,000 followers, that # will be 50

- If you have 100,000 followers, that # will be 100

- If you have 250,000 followers, that # will be 250

Contingent upon your engagement level, you will have an alternate CPM esteem.

Stage 3: Plug such information (engagement rate and CPM esteem) into the recipe:

CPM VALUE * (# of followers/1000) = cost per post.

Model: You have an engagement rate of 2.5% and 70,000 followers

$5 * (70,000/1000) = $350 per post.

The Rate for Insta Stories utilizing CPM.

On the off chance that your Insta stories have an alternate engagement rate than your changeless posts, you're going to need to do that equation separately. You'll figure the engagement rate for your stories, and afterward utilize the proper CPM Value and duplicate it times the # of followers/1000, much the same as you did previously. Once more, we generally prescribe making bundles and giving limits. For instance, "1 post will cost X sum, yet in the event that you buy 3 posts, you will get a 30% rebate." And you ought to consistently send the brand a contact sheet of the entirety of the photos you took, that way you can charge for them separately on the off chance that they are keen on buying extra photos from your roll.

Eventually, we realize everybody is at various stages and has various qualities so we can't state there is just a single method to value yourself yet we needed to assist you with excursion by exhibiting various alternatives. Toward the day's end, just you know how you became your following and how genuine your engagement is and when working with brands, you need to feel certain that your evaluating is reasonable.

EARNING WITH INSTAGRAM SPONSORSHIP.

Influenccrs receive the respect and praise frpm their audience and receive financial rewards from their sponsors. So it is not surprising that many people strive to reach this level of influence and receive the kudos that accompany the title. In most cases, people by pure luck do not become influential people. They work to build the confidence of their audience and rise in the niche. And as they gain reputation and status, they can see a lucrative Instagram sponsorship prize.

Build Your Reach and Influence

You may think you the photos you post on Instagram are the most eye-catching and attractive images on the net. But they are of little value if nobody sees them. Likewise, you will be of little value to a brand if nobody sees any sponsored posts you make on their behalf. It is easy to be confident and create an attractive Instagram account. But that doesn't make you an influencer. There is one glaring requirement for people to consider you an influencer. You have to actually influence a sizeable number of followers. You need sufficient support from many people to react to your posts. To be an influencer, you need both reach and engagement. You will not receive Instagram sponsorship without these two essential qualities.

Instagram Influencer Sponsored Post Money Calculator:

The Influencer Marketing Hub can give you a sign of your potential worth as far as Instagram Sponsorship. It adjusts this requirement for followers with the truth that the more followers you have, the harder it is to keep them all locked in. This is one reason that micro-influencers are frequently more successful than superstars. The reach of micro-influencers might be not exactly their celebrity counterparts, yet their followers will in general be considerably more intense supporters.

This makes coherent sense. While you might be somewhat keen on following some celebrity, you presumably give less belief to their suppositions than you do to people you perceive as specialists in a field. Additionally, it is a lot more straightforward for a micro-influencer to speak with an adherent in a two-manner discussion than it is a celebrity. The Instagram Influencer Sponsored Post Money Calculator perceives this, giving higher commitment weightings to micro-influencers (and even ordinary people) than the purported genius VIPs. You need to adjust the greater reach of bigger accounts with the littler commitment rates.

Regularly, the best influencers online are people with a mid-run following, i.e., certifiable micro-influencers. Thusly, on the off chance that you set yourself with an objective to procure an open to living with Instagram sponsorship, you have to initially set up yourself as a micro-influencer. Brands at first centered around people with high adherent numbers – if not certifiable big names, at any rate the large scale influencers who are geniuses on a particular theme. All the more as of late, in any case, brands have found that reach isn't all that matters. High commitment can be similarly, if not increasingly, basic when finding people who can spread the message.

Focus on a Dedicated Niche

The most success Instagrammers concentrate their energies on establishing expertise in a particular niche. A smorgasbord of posts on a range of topics may appear genuine, but they do not build you a devoted audience. The bulk of the people who will follow your Instagram account will do so because they are interested in the images you post and want to hear what you have to say. They share, like, and otherwise interact with your posts if they believe they can trust you. You are effectively building your brand in that niche.

Whether you always post images about a particular topic, highlight one specific part of your life, or even just consistently display the same type of picture, you are building your Instagram standing.

In an ideal world, a brand pays those influencers whose followers are a perfect match for their target sales base. So, if you want to earn Instagram sponsorship, you need to build up a following of the type of people who would like the same kinds of products. There is little point having too diverse a range of followers, as this does not advantage potential sponsors.

For example, you might love shoes. You may take note of shoe trends, and possibly wear the latest shoes yourself. In that case, you will want to post images of trendy footwear, so other shoe lovers know they can rely on you to keep them informed if current shoe trends. You want to build up a following of fellow shoe lovers. The first step to gaining Instagram sponsorship is to create your personal brand. What interests you enough to warrant becoming an expert? The vast majority of your posts need to show images related to this topic.

Work to a Consistent Posting Schedule

Your followers will begin to look forward to your posts. You need to build up their trust, so you should set up some form of schedule to emphasize your reliability. Instagram's algorithm also rewards people who post consistently. This is one of the factors that Instagram considers when creating a user's feed. Once brands begin to look at you, they will notice your posting practices, too. They will feed more confident working with somebody who posts regular updates and demonstrates that they can be relied upon. CoSchedule analyzed 14 studies into social sharing and came up with the ultimate number of posts you should make each day on each social network. They found that significant brands share on Instagram 1-2 post per day, sometimes up to 3 times. Adobe recommends even more – up to ten posts per day. Of course, influencers have a more dedicated audience than brands do, so influencers will typically post even more frequently.

Don't Forget Engagement

Influencers do far more than merely post their favorite pictures on Instagram. They actively engage with their followers. If you find that your followers aren't regularly liking, sharing, and commenting on your posts, then you are doing something wrong. This is the main reason why it is pointless to buy followers. It is unlikely that any followers you gain by this method have any interest in your posts. They are unlikely to even see them. With zero engagement, they are certainly not going to take your advice to buy any sponsored products. Brands are far more likely to sponsor an Instagrammer with a small but active audience than they are somebody with a sizeable unresponsive set of followers.

Use Relevant Hashtags with Every Post

Instagram uses extremely good hashtags. In fact, most shared posts on Instagram use more hashtags than you think on other platforms, such as Facebook or Twitter. Instagram allows you to embed up to 30 hashtags in a post. It's usually used by so many people, but it's common to include 10 to 15 hashtags in a message.

A recent change has made it possible for people to follow hashtags. This means that the messages you create contain the appropriate hashtags, even if they have not already been followed. Instagram now rewards posts that include concise and relevant hashtags. But you should definitely stick to the relevant hashtags. Users have the option to select their publication and click on "View this title". If many users do this, Instagram may activate a red flag in its content. This emphasizes that you have to customize your hashtags for each message. You cannot copy and paste a generic set into every message you post.

Preempt Future Relationships by Tagging Brands You Admire

One way to become visible to the brand is to mark it in some of your messages. Obviously, you just want to spam it. But every time you publish a publication containing the relevant brand, @ lies in the description of your publication. If you do it often enough, the brand can share your images. This will make your name visible to people using social media accounts. Of course, you have to be strategic here. In many ways, this sounds like an unwanted labor lawsuit. There is no point in tagging in a blurry image that shows a brand with good light. He could even intentionally launch a brand by asking him to share his message in exchange for some of his pictures.

Create a Personalized Package to Pitch Brands

After gathering a considerable number of devoted followers, you can consider presenting the case for the brand and thus offer services to your influencer. Be sure to adjust your tone to each brand you want to work with. Nothing seems worse than the general tone. Most people start working with small brands before the trucking industry wants to partner with them. Look into some brands in your area and start creating a lot for toddlers. It will be much easier to get started with these companies, though the payments are of course more modest. You can start the process by interacting with brand publications. Use your custom hashtags. Your goal at this stage is simply to gain recognition. By doing this, you can send them a direct message telling them how much you like your brand and suggesting the benefits of possible collaboration. Again, be sure to personalize these messages.

If they reply to your direct messages, you can email them, preferably to your social media manager, if you can find the correct email address. In the next step, you should send them a cover letter informing them of you. This should include your Instagram subscriber information, your niche experience, relevant statistics (or subscriber samples and engagement data), and any notable achievements that have enhanced your reputation as an expert in your field. Finally, in your presentation, you have to tell them why you will make the right decision for your brand, or the benefits you can get.

Consider Working with a Platform

Another option is to sign up for one of the influencer marketing platforms. You should look for a platform that gives you the ability to become a member, not an algorithm-based platform. The platforms generally accept people who, in their view, share high quality content with decent monitoring (and dedication). Depending on the platform, you might need to wait for your brand to be addressed or you may request a specific campaign.

Be Clear About What a Brand Expects

If you figure out how to be picked for Instagram sponsorship, it is pivotal that you have clear desires for the brand. You are probably not going to get paid for your work on the off chance that you keep on creating what the brand don't need. You should know the measure of productions paid for by the brand and the kind of content you hope to get ready. Would you be able to make the content yourself or will the brand give the content? On the off chance that this is the last case, you should be a decent counterpart for your followers and sound legitimate. A few brands would like to have a voice in article content, others give you more opportunity. Correspondingly, you should watch that particular hashtags ought to be utilized. Remember that the brand make the principles for sponsored posts. They are probably not going to need to work with you some other time on the off chance that they don't care for the messages you post. It will intently look at the breaks down that show the adequacy of the messages you compose. Finally, remember that Instagram currently anticipates that compelling individuals should submit to the FTC support exposure arrangement. Instagram now has a particular tool that you should utilize each time you distribute a sponsored post.

WAYS TO EARN MONEY USING INSTAGRAM

1. Affiliate Marketing

Affiliate marketing is fundamentally when you promote an item and get paid per sale. You'll frequently observe some bloggers doing this with sidebar flags advancing their partners (affiliates), or even through explicit item roused posts. All things considered, it's very little extraordinary with Instagram. With Instagram, you post appealing pictures featuring their items and drive sales through your affiliate URL (this ought to be given by your affiliate).There are many organizations you can work with here. Here are a few:

- Sharesale: Find organizations you need to work with, pursue their affiliate program, get approved at that point start advancing. In certain projects, it's easier to get approved on the off chance that you have a blog or website.

- Ebates: Refer people that affection bargains and limits, at that point get commission.

- Stylinity: great for design bloggers. At the point when people shop utilizing your link, you'll get commission.

You can put your affiliate URL on your inscriptions or on your profile. You can either utilize bitly.com to abbreviate and modify your affiliate link OR you can connect your blog and Instagram profile so when people buy through your link, you get a sale. It truly couldn't be easier. This kind of marketing is particularly mainstream with clothing on Instagram, as you can post your "OOTD" (outfit of the day) with the affiliate link sending followers to your full outfit subtleties. For those associated with the movement business (or basically those that affection to travel – ahem, we all!), you could attempt to set up and use affiliate marketing when participating in surveys for inns and scenes. Essentially immediate followers to book through your link! It's additionally great for excellence bloggers, as you can welcome people to "shop the look." These techniques are subtler and, in that capacity, more viable than an immediate sales type pitch.

2. Make Sponsored Posts (Find Sponsors!)

Instagram clients with connected followings can win additional cash by making unique sponsored content for brands. More or less, a bit of sponsored content on Instagram is a photograph or video that features an item or a brand. These posts are joined by captions that may incorporate branded hashtags, @mentions, or links. Brands don't normally require a proper brand ambassadorship for makers of sponsored content, however it's not unexpected to for them to tap certain influencers for content over and over. Notwithstanding, it's significant that any brands or products you promote are a solid match for your very own picture on Instagram. The thought is to show off brands that you can by and by get behind, and to show your followers how that brand fits into your way of life.

• TapInfluence is a great tool for Instagram makers who are searching for open doors for sponsored content, and it removes the guesswork from the way toward lining up with brands. You make a profile that portrays you and the idea of your content, and brands who are keen on working with you will welcome you to programs.

• Ifluenz is another simple tool as you can peruse coordinating accessible crusades made by an assortment of brands and legitimately promote the ones you like.

3. Sell your photos

An undeniable one, unquestionably? Why not utilize Instagram for it sole reason… to showcase your photography? In case you're an expert (or beginner yet sharp!) picture taker, Instagram is a great method to publicize and sell your shots to either people or offices. Add a watermark to your snaps and utilize the captions to list all selling subtleties in a brief way. As usual, make sure that you have a functioning nearness with the goal that the correct kind of accounts are tailing you. Utilize fitting hashtags to pull people towards your shots and get a discussion moving with compelling photography organizations. There are additionally a couple of sites that you can use to really put your Instagram photos available to be purchased, including:

- Twenty20
- Community Foap

4. Promote your business, products or services

In the event that you maintain your very own business, at that point Instagram needs to hold an essential spot in your marketing lattice. In the event that you sell products, use it to post excellent shots that can't be found on your website. Here are some inventive approaches to promote your products or services:

• Behind the scenes: "In the background" type pictures will in general be colossally prominent – picture lovely carefully assembled cleansers being blessing wrapped, adornments being sorted out or tasty cakes straight out of the stove. It's engaging and adds a specific realness to what you're doing… and people love that.

- Your customers' photos: Linked to this is the utilization of User Generated Content on your account. Get customers to share their pictures of your products and re-gram (download "Repost for Instagram" application to repost your customers' photos). This is a demonstrated fruitful strategy for selling and would make a great expansion to your account. It additionally calls for you to fire up your own unique hashtag which you would then be able to promote to every one of your customers: it's a truly smooth approach to make yourself stand apart from the group. For instance, White Castle requests that their customers use #MyCrave to their photos. Presently when they see them utilizing that hashtag, they can repost (or regram) their photos to their Instagram account.

- Infographics + selective offers. You can likewise showcase your services through Instagram with sweet infographics and selective offers. Utilizing Instagram to include extraordinary offers is likewise a great tool to up your devotee consider it's a reward they won't find anyplace else.

The splendid thing about utilizing Instagram to promote your business is you can get mega inventive with it. Think outside about the container and truly use it furthering your full potential benefit. You're certain to see the sales flying in.

5. Sell your Instagram account

Had enough of Instagram? Ready to move on? Well, you'll be happy to know that all your hard work hasn't gone to waste. You can actually sell your Instagram account if (for whatever reason) you can no longer manage it. There's a few site that support you with this, two of the best being:

- Fame swap
- Viral accounts

TOP INSTAGRAM INFLUENCERS

Now that you know who an Instagram influencer is, the types of influencers available and what they are all about, let's look at who the famous Instagram influencers are these days. Check out this list of the most widely followed online influencers in different business fields to give you an overview of the current Instagram landscape and help you understand what kind of content is mostly consumed in this platform.

Instagram

With over 302 million followers and counting, perhaps expectedly, Instagram's official page is the most followed. The account is used primarily throughout the platform to showcase various developers that work for them and all about their work life.

Cristiano Ronaldo

With 169 million followers, Cristiano Ronaldo Soccer player Cristiano Ronaldo made his way to second place on the list of top influencers of Instagram. He is loved by teeming football fans all over the world who can't get tired of comparing with Messi. Ronaldo"s page has majorly soccer-related posts, but on a few occasions he uploads posts about his personal life, including his children, vacation and his mansion

Kim Kardashian West

Popular American reality TV personality and socialite Kimberly Kardashian West popularly Known for their reality series on E-network has over time dropped in rankings in. She fell to No. 6 and has over 104 million followers at the moment. She's the Kardashian-Jenner clan's most famous member on Instagram, posting mostly about herself, her family members, and her KKW Beauty brand.

Beyoncé

In 2019, on the list of Instagram accounts with the most followers, Beyoncé fell to eighth, with more than 128 million current followers. Her posts have always had a high level of commitment. She shares posts with more than a million likes and many comments per post. Usually, Beyoncé posts pictures of herself or her family. A few years ago, she used her popular Instagram platform to reveal that she was pregnant with Jay-Z husband twins, which made headlines all over the world.

Leo Messi (Lionel Messi)

The Argentine soccer player, Lionel Messi, and best footballer of the year 2019; According to FIFA rankings boasts of over with 120 million followers. He currently holds the ninth place on Instagram rankings. He usually posts about soccer, although he sometimes posts about his family and events.

INFLUENCERS FOR DROPSHIPPING

Who would have thought, right?! Instagram is indeed a market place once you have your niche carved out! There is presently a vast market for dropshipping influencers from Instagram where aspiring entrepreneurs can check through for latest information in the world of drop shipping. These are businessmen who have earned quite a great deal of support in the business world and are focused explicitly on dropshipping business. Here is a list for showing a few of them.

Gabriel Beltran

With more than 73,000 followers, Gabriel Beltran is one of the biggest dropshipping influencers on Instagram. He usually posts business-related motivational content and lifestyle material.

Ryan Melnick

He is quite an experienced young entrepreneur. He often posts about his life and projects and has over 12,000 followers, and unlike other entrepreneurs, he holds weekly live Q&A sessions, which drives massive engagement from people with mutual interests.

Anthony Mastellone

Anthony Mastellone (also known to be Tony Mast) is yet another specialist in the Shopify business community, who used Instagram to build his target audience organically. He frequently shares some business tips and inspirational quotes to his more than 7,700 followers. He one of the most information-centred dropshipping influencers of Instagram and loved by his followers.

INSTAGRAM INFLUENCERS RELATED TO FOOD AND NUTRITION.

Instagram has given a platform for food influencers all over the world to share their passion for food, nutritional tips, and recipes for various kinds of dishes, with their followers. These influencers range from world-renowned chefs to small-scale café owners, or even people just motivated to share their food journey and experience.

Based on their popularity and because everybody loves food, they have gained a following. For every "foodie" around you, you will discover they have a food influencer they are passionate about. Here we've compiled for you some of the top current Instagram influencers related to food and nutrition.

Jamie Oliver

On Instagram, Jamie Oliver British celebrity chef and restaurateur Jamie Oliver has over 7.2 million followers, placing him one of the most popular food influencers. Jamie Oliver is known for his restaurant chain, television shows, and cookbooks. His Instagram is filled with delicious-looking food pictures as well as occasional private images.

Natalie Mortimer (The Modern Proper)

The ladies behind The Modern Proper are Natalie Mortimer and Holly Erickson. We are now gaining a lot of attention with more than 150,000 followers after being finalists for Saveur's Best Home-Cooked Food Blog in 2016. They were praised in preparing quick and delicious meals for their modern approach, and that has earned them a place in the hearts of many food lovers all over the world.

TOP PHOTOGRAPHY INFLUENCERS

Instagram Photography's Top Photography Influencers is another category that exploded on Instagram. This makes perfect sense–after all, Instagram is mainly an application for photography.

Here are two top Instagram's photography influencers.

Paul Nicklen

Paul Nicklen, with a record 5.4 million followers, is one of Instagram's top photography influencers. A "National Geographic" blogger, Nicklen usually posts photos related to nature and adventure.

Chris Burkard.

Burkard is another nature and wildlife photographer who has gained 3.4 million followers on Instagram. His unique, high-quality nature shots attract tens of thousands of likes per post and hundreds of comments.

FASHION INFLUENCERS

Instagram Fashion's top fashion influencers are incredibly popular with Instagram. There are plenty of fashion-focusing Instagram influencers who post pictures and videos about the trending fashion for different seasons of the year. If you are a fashion lover, I"m glad to let you know that you have a plethora of options when it comes to choosing your fashion muse. Here are some of Instagram's top fashion influencers today.

Alexa Chung

Alexa Chung is a vital member of the fashion community of Instagram. She has one of the most followed style pages on the internet with 3.3 million followers. While she has a separate account specifically for her fashion line, there are many fashion-related posts on her account, as well.

Julia Engel

Julia Engel is another prominent influencer of Instagram fashion with more than 1.2 million followers. She blogs about Gal Meets Glam, her dress line, and shares other content related to style.

Marketing influencers from Instagram is one of the best strategies you can use to create awareness for your brand. As an influencer, you can potentially make thousands overnight without lifting a finger by exploiting the power of influencer marketing on any niche that you may be interested in.

And as you've seen, Instagram has all sorts of influencers from different walks of life. It is time to explore the niche(s) you find interesting, follow them, and even check out what these Instagram Influencers how use various tactics of advertisement to generate leads and traffic for multiple brands all over the world.

Instagram is one of today's most popular social media networks, and it is growing steadily every day, so it is high time you tap into the vast market and create brand name for yourself or at least join a community to learn more. As a brand, If you are not targeting influencer marketing on Instagram, your brand may be lacking a great deal and might not be able to compete with other leading brands in the nearest future, which is why you must ensure you build a successful Instagram account for your brand.

All the tips you need for that are in the preceding pages of this book. Instagram Influencer marketing is one of the easiest ways to spend your marketing budget, and you can be guaranteed to see hundreds or even thousands of people flocking to your product generating quality leads, conversion and an increased ROI.

Do not go yet; One last thing yo do…

If you enjoyed this book or found it useful, I'd be very grateful if you'd post a short review on **Amazon**. Your support does make a difference, and I read all the reviews personally so I can get your feedback and make this book even better.

Thanks again for your support!

© Copyright 2019 by **JEREMY BARTON**

All rights reserved

Made in the USA
San Bernardino, CA
27 December 2019

62413091R00155